OLD-TIMERS' STORIES
FROM AA GRAPEVINE

VOICES OF LONG-TERM
Sobriety

BOOKS PUBLISHED BY AA GRAPEVINE, INC.

The Language of the Heart (& eBook)
The Best of the Grapevine Volume I (& eBook)
The Best of Bill (& eBook)
Thank You for Sharing
Spiritual Awakenings (& eBook)
I Am Responsible: The Hand of AA
The Home Group: Heartbeat of AA (& eBook)
Emotional Sobriety — The Next Frontier (& eBook)
Spiritual Awakenings II (& eBook)
In Our Own Words: Stories of Young AAs in Recovery (& eBook)
Beginners' Book (& eBook)
Voices of Long-Term Sobriety (& eBook)
A Rabbit Walks Into A Bar
Step by Step — Real AAs, Real Recovery (& eBook)
Emotional Sobriety II — The Next Frontier (& eBook)
Young & Sober (& eBook)
Into Action (& eBook)
Happy, Joyous & Free (& eBook)
One on One (& eBook)
No Matter What (& eBook)
Grapevine Daily Quote Book (& eBook)
Sober & Out (& eBook)
Forming True Partnerships (& eBook)
Our Twelve Traditions (& eBook)
Making Amends (& eBook)
Voices of Women in AA (& eBook)

IN SPANISH

El lenguaje del corazón
Lo mejor de Bill (& eBook)
El grupo base: Corazón de AA
Lo mejor de La Viña
Felices, alegres y libres (& eBook)
Un día a la vez (& eBook)

IN FRENCH

Le langage du coeur
Les meilleurs articles de Bill
Le Groupe d'attache: Le battement du coeur des AA
En tête à tête (& eBook)
Heureux, joyeux et libres (& eBook)

OLD-TIMERS' STORIES
FROM AA GRAPEVINE

VOICES OF LONG-TERM
Sobriety

AAGRAPEVINE,Inc.
NEW YORK, NEW YORK
www.aagrapevine.org

ISBN: 978-0-933685-77-2

AA PREAMBLE

Alcoholics Anonymous is a fellowship of men and women who
share their experience, strength and hope with each other that
they may solve their common problem and help others to
recover from alcoholism.

The only requirement for membership is a desire to stop
drinking. There are no dues or fees for AA membership; we are
self-supporting through our own contributions. AA is not allied
with any sect, denomination, politics, organization or institution; does not wish to engage in any controversy, neither
endorses nor opposes any causes.

Our primary purpose is to stay sober and help other alcoholics
to achieve sobriety.

CONTENTS

A Note To Our Readers

SECTION ONE: The Jumping—Off Place   *11*

A Power Greater Than Compulsion. . . . . *May 1992*   *12*

Absolutely Richard. . . . . *April 1998*   *14*

From Handcuffs to Hope. *February 2001*   *17*

The Perfect Curve. . . . . *November 2004*   *20*

A Real War Story. . . . . *April 2002*   *23*

From Rags to Riches. . . . . *January 2005*   *26*

SECTION TWO: Living History   *31*

Sober for Thirty Years. . . . . *May 1968*   *32*

The Seven-Day Test. . . . . *November 2001*   *33*

Practice These Principles. . . . . *November 1997*   *36*

From Wagon Trains to Jets. . . . . *June 1995*   *39*

It Works for Me. . . . . *September 2007*   *46*

The Fishing Guide, the Bartender, and Me. . . . . . . *September 1996*   *50*

A Place of Either/Or. . . . . *April 1999*   *54*

How AA Came to Geneva, Nebraska. . . . . *July 2001*   *58*

SECTION THREE: A Journey Not A Destination   *63*

The Quest for Spirituality. . . . . *March 2000*   *64*

Taking Gratitude for Granted. . . . . *May 2000*   *65*

The Bottom of the Glass. . . . . *March 2009*   *66*

Weeding out the Crabgrass. . . . . *August 1984*   *69*

What AA Means to Me. . . . . *October 1998*   *71*

You Can Always Tell Another Alcoholic. . . . . *July 2000*   *72*

A Seat, A Cup of Coffee, and Lots of Love. . . . . *August 1998*   *74*

Gratitude . . . . *September 1979*   *78*

Old-Timers in the Making. *December 1992*   *82*

SECTION FOUR: The Challenge Of Change 87

Facing the Future Without the Froth. . . . . *April 1996* 88

Freedom from Alcohol. . . . . *February 1992* ... 90

Portals of the Program. . . . . *December 2005* ... 92

The Same Chance I Had. . . . . *September 2001* ... 95

... And the Wisdom to Know the Difference. . . . . . *June 1994* 97

Anything and Everything Except Sobriety. . . . . *May 1998* 100

Who's the Boss?. . . . . *December 1993* ... 102

SECTION FIVE: Interviews 107

A Living Big Book. . . . . *May 2006* 108

The Real Thing. . . . . *February 2001* ... 112

Dateline, Alaska. . . . . *August 2000* 118

Reflections on 28 Years of Experience at our GSO. . *September 2002* ... 122

A Fine Old Tree. . . . . *June 2006* 126

SECTION SIX: Making It New 133

Taking the Time to Listen. . . . . *December 1997* ... 134

An Old-Timer's Checklist . . . . *June 1989* 136

Why I Keep Coming Back. . . . . *May 2001* 137

Online and Active. . . . . *May 2003* 141

A New Way of Looking at Life. . . . . *April 1981* 143

Reciprocal Strength. . . . . *January 1998* ... 145

THE LAST WORD Words of Wisdom . . . . *May 1998* 149

Twelve Steps 150

Twelve Traditions 151

About AA and AA Grapevine 152

—⌇∿∿⌇—

A NOTE TO OUR READERS

This collection presents 42 stories from old-timers about how they hit bottom and got sober, as well as vivid descriptions of the early days of AA. But colorful histories are only part of the book. Old-timers have a wealth of lived experience to share with the rest of us. They've stayed sober through good times and bad by depending on the Steps and their Higher Powers. They've learned how to avoid complacency and renew their committment to sobriety. They're here to tell us, "Life happens: don't drink, go to meetings, trust the principles of AA, and be willing to stay willing." They have the gift of perspective and know that sobriety is a journey, not a destination—whether the traveler is a newcomer just heading out or a longtimer who has had his passport stamped many times.

A wry comment AA old-timers sometimes make, when they're asked how to accumulate sober years, is: Don't drink and don't die. But how to be an old-timer and remain engaged, contented and productive? That's another story—or stories. Read on.

The Jumping-Off Place

"He cannot picture life without alcohol. Some day he will
be unable to imagine life either with alcohol or without it.
Then he will know loneliness such as few do. He will be at
the jumping-off place. He will wish for the end."

"A Vision for You," Alcoholics Anonymous

T he phrase "jumping-off place" has two interesting meanings.
The first is a remote place, somewhere far from human
civilization. For active alcoholics that represents a condition
that's desperate, lonely and hopeless. At the end, the drunk feels cut off
from the human community, if only in her own mind.

But the second meaning brings us hope after despair: a jumping-off
place is also one where a journey begins.

The old-timers in this section describe how they came to that dark
place where there seemed nowhere else to go, and how they found AA and
the adventure began.

——∽∾∽——

A Power Greater Than Compulsion
May 1992

AUGUST 5, 1960 marks the end of what I pray was my last drunken episode. It was a two-day affair, spent mostly in a blackout. It occurred after eleven months of meetings and so-called "sobriety," triggered by a resentment I'd been nursing for several weeks against a coworker. This was the catalyst for a long overdue, genuine bottom. I was nearly twenty-eight.

I passed out in a restaurant booth, head on a table, in the most grungy, low-life bar in town—par for me by then. When I came to, the clock on the wall read 9:15 AM—or was it PM? Bleary eyes slowly focused on the half-glass of warm beer in front of me; there it sat, the symbol and true cause of all the misery and wreckage in my life.

A sickening knowledge struck me full on: alcohol no longer worked. My best friend and reliable source of comfort for years was now a mortal enemy out to kill me.

A power greater than compulsion prevented me from finishing that stale beer. Staggering out of the bar into the darkness, I somehow found my beat-up sedan, crawled into it, fired the engine, and hand over one eye, headed for home and family, ten miles away over dark, winding back roads.

God watches over drunks and fools; the car and I arrived safely, not at my house, but at my neighbor's, a young lady who was sober in AA (I probably had some idea that I was heaven's gift to women). That's where my wife found me, drunk on the sofa, slobbering and incoherent. She drove me home, wrestled me inside, and I fell into bed, out like a light.

Next morning, I awoke nearly paralyzed, feeling as if the life force had drained out of my body during the night; I couldn't get up. Realization flooded in: So this was what the old-timers meant about progression—I'd been sober for eleven months but my drinking had gotten worse.

It's all over this time, I thought, convinced, God help me, that I was going to die right there. (A year earlier, I'd been on a terrible binge for ten weeks and not felt like this—just a big hangover and five days of the shakes.)

Disappointment, hurt, and sadness clouded my wife's pretty face: Eleven months of hopes, dreams, and rebuilding were torn from her grasp, one more time. Our four little ones wouldn't come near me; Daddy was "sick" and all messed up—again.

Lying there helpless, I knew I'd never be able to drink again and stay alive; I (finally!) surrendered, and accepted my alcoholism without reservation. Wonder of wonders, a new peace came over me. Later that day, still weak and shaky but willing, I phoned my not-so-surprised sponsor; he drove over and took my sick body, mind, and soul to a meeting.

Thirty years later, my Higher Power still grants me very clear memories of that last morning-after scene; they keep my "forgetter" from kicking in. Thanks to my God, AA, and the Twelve Steps, sobriety has become the "easier, softer way" for me. Life in sobriety rolls onward with its ups and downs, successes and failures, joys and pains. But compared to the old drinking or on-the-wagon days, and those uptight hellish eleven months of "dryness," it's a picnic.

Norm W.

Magalia, California

FROM "AN ENGLISH GENTLEMAN"

December 1999

When I got to my lowest point, I knew I was beaten, and I cried out in desperation. Right then and there, I had a white-flash spiritual experience and was struck sober on the spot.

Plucking up my courage, I went to my first AA meeting. I got there early and hid behind a bush outside the building, so that I could see what alcoholics looked like. An old car rattled around the corner and shuddering to a halt, disgorged its contents of disconcertingly happy people.

After they'd all gone inside, I waited behind the bush till the lights in the meeting room went on, and then I crept in, hoping not to be noticed. I needn't have worried. I was made very welcome indeed. A dear old lady wearing a tweed suit and a clear-eyed expression made me half a cup of tea, gave me some leaflets, and suggested that I sit down and listen. As the meeting progressed, my hopes began to rise, and I went home that night for the first time with hope in my heart and a real feeling of freedom. I had a fatal malady, but there was a solution to my problem. Since that night, the compulsion to drink was lifted and has never returned. I make a conscious effort to keep it simple, because the simpler I make it, the happier I become. I don't need to hide in bushes anymore (that bush incidentally, has become a thirty-foot tree).

Keith J. M.

Clevedon, Somerset

—◊◊◊—

Absolutely Richard
April 1998

MY STORY BEGAN on January 27, 1938, a cold snowy day in Syracuse, New York. My first remembrance of alcohol was my father coming home at eight every morning after working all night in the steel mill to put food on our table and a roof over our heads. He'd reach up to the cupboard, take down his bottle of whiskey and pour himself a strong one. Then he'd look down at me and say, "This is Daddy's medicine. This makes Daddy feel good." Both he and my mother drank every day, and I got the notion at an early age that alcohol helped whatever ailed you.

During my high school years I never drank because I didn't want to be like my parents. I had an inner feeling that if I added alcohol to the severe emotional mood swings I was already having, it would be disastrous.

This changed in October 1956 when I was a freshman at Syracuse University. On the very day that Don Larsen pitched his perfect game for the New York Yankees, I attended a fraternity rush party and had to chugalug a pitcher of beer. As that beer went down my throat I felt the wonderful warm glow my father had told me about years ago. With my first taste of alcohol, I had a blackout and passed out.

I didn't draw a sober breath for the next four years. I finished classes (the ones I went to) about noon. Then my drinking began with a couple of Manhattans, flowing into eight or ten bottles of beer, and finishing around eleven o'clock with a couple of whiskey-and-gingers. Then I passed out. The next day I got up and started all over again. I did this five days a week with variations on the weekends.

At the end of my senior year, after four years of daily blackouts and one half-hearted attempt at suicide, I contacted a young priest at the Cathedral of the Immaculate Conception. His name was Father Joseph. I was told that he'd graduated from a very prestigious prep school in New England and gone through a year at Yale before becoming a priest. I felt that this man had the intelligence to understand me. After listening for an hour to the story of my drinking, he took from his desk drawer a pamphlet from Johns Hopkins University called "The Twenty Questions." He asked me each question. I answered yes to about ten of them. Then he said to me, "It says here that if you answered yes to three of these, you're an alcoholic."

I was stunned. I thought this man was intelligent. I was ready to leave immediately. Then Father Joseph had the nerve to tell me he wanted me to meet an alcoholic that very evening. Well, I thought, maybe it would be good to see what one looked like, so in case I ever met one at a bar, I could stay away from him.

He sent me to the Twenty-Four-Hour Club, which was above Gotch Carr's Grill on Warren Street. I stood outside the bar for half an hour because I didn't want anyone to see me going up those stairs to the club. Finally I opened the door and a waft of smoke hit me in the face. Through the haze of smoke I saw that there was a guy waiting at the top of the stairs to greet me. "I thought you weren't coming up, kid. I've been waiting for you for over an hour!" His named, it turned out, was Emerson.

He told me that it isn't how much you drink, or when or where you drink, that determines whether you've crossed the invisible line into alcoholism. The determining factor was very simple: what happens to a person's personality after he takes alcohol into his system. In my case, it felt like I was alcoholic from my first sip. I never had a period of social drinking.

I thanked Emerson for his information. I knew that I was pretty crazy, but I wasn't ready to admit that I was alcoholic. So I began seeing a psychiatrist. I also got a job teaching fifth grade in a school district near Syracuse. For the next two years I never drank while in class, but I did come in with a hangover every day. I'm not proud of this. I attended one or two AA meetings during the period I was seeing the psychiatrist once a week.

Finally, in April 1962, an event happened that changed my life. I awoke one morning feeling fluish, sweaty, and very sick. Then an awful conviction took hold, that I had stayed home from school the day before and hadn't called a substitute teacher. My God, I thought, how am I going to talk my way out of this one? I went to school and waited outside the principal's door like an errant little boy. When the door opened, I faced this man and asked him if I could speak to him for a moment. He asked me what the problem was. "Well," I began, "I was very sick yesterday with a fever and the flu, which is why I made such an awful mistake." "Refresh my memory," the principal went on. "What happened yesterday?"

I winced. "I didn't come to work, and I forgot to call a substitute teacher. I'm very sorry, and it will never happen again."

Then he looked in my eyes very carefully and said, "Dick, you were here yesterday."

"Oh," I said, backing out of the office. "It must have been a bad dream."

Before the first of June my principal called me into the office and said that he

---

"FROM MAKE-BELIEVE TO BELIEF"

June 1981

When I read in the Big Book (after asking God to bring some calmness to my life) that I could find happiness, power, peace, and a sense of direction, and that God did not make too hard demands on those that earnestly seek him, I began to be encouraged. Reading further in our Big Book, I was relieved to learn that I didn't have to believe, only be willing to believe. This I could do. I couldn't believe, but I made believe—and came to believe. When I surrendered, the battle was over. I finally realized that I did not drink because I wanted to—I drank because I had to. This leads me to think that we alcoholics do not try to stop drinking until we discover that we can't stop drinking. Then we must ask for help. I asked for help from a fellowship of lovely people who accepted me, not for what I had been, nor for what I might become, but for what I was: a suffering, dying alcoholic. When I drank, I made numerous trips to mental institutions, jails, and just plain nowhere. Today, I am ten years happily sober in the Fellowship. I have found the God of my understanding and gotten everything I need and most of what I want. I'm glad I surrendered.

B. B.

Charleston, West Virginia

---

didn't want me in his school next year, but that he wouldn't blackball me if I could find another job teaching in the district.

By the time I was twenty-four, I was losing my career, an internist had told me I'd probably lose my stomach, and a psychiatrist had said I might kill myself from depression. I had nowhere to turn. So on June 22, 1962, after drinking all day with some teachers, I called a man named Tom whom I'd met at an AA meeting the previous New Year's Eve. I'd noticed he was wearing a college ring and that impressed me. I asked if he'd pick me up from where I was drinking and take me to the Friday night Dewitt Group. Then I told everyone I was drinking with that an alcoholic was coming to take me to an AA meeting, and this produced a great amount of interest. My fellow teachers were eager to meet this alcoholic. So, when the doorbell rang at seven-thirty, Tom was faced with eight to ten teachers who were pretty well sloshed by then. (Needless to say he continues to remind me of this event today.)

On the way home after the meeting, I asked Tom if he thought I could make the program. "Absolutely, Richard," he said. "Absolutely." I asked him the same question a couple of more times. Each time he answered, "Absolutely, Richard, absolutely."

The next morning I woke up, and from that day to this, I have not had a compulsion to drink.

The past thirty-five years have brought all of the joy, happiness, and sadness that happen to anyone over a span of time. I have a wonderful wife, two beautiful children, as well as a retirement plaque from teaching thirty-three years in various school districts in New York and California. I'm an active member of my home groups, the Sunday morning Spiritual Progress Group and the Roxas Mens' Group. I attend at least three meetings a week. I've served on the county alcoholism advisory board. I do volunteer work every week in a second-grade classroom. My wife and I travel frequently. I've always loved poetry and now have time to write each day. Despite many health problems I'm able to walk on the beach, where I commune with my Higher Power.

The spirit of Alcoholics Anonymous has been with me for thirty-five years: for better or for worse, for richer or for poorer, in sickness and in health. I know at the moment of death the same Higher Power who gave me my sobriety will be there to greet me and to take me to another level of being, another level of consciousness, and another level of sobriety.

Richard S.
Santa Cruz, California

—◦◦◦—

From Handcuffs to Hope
February 2001

I WAS A low-bottom drunk, having hit as low a bottom as any drunk can hit and live to tell about it.

I was a patient in the state mental hospital, having been committed to that desolate place by my mother. She had been called by the police to come and get me.

I had been fished out of Lake Erie by the Coast Guard after my latest suicide attempt, put in handcuffs because my behavior swung from sweet and docile one minute, waving and smiling at the crowds gathered for the regatta, to being violent and uncontrollable in an instant. On land, I was handcuffed to a metal table. I was completely crazed from alcohol. When my mother tried to get me to go with her, I started screaming obscenities at her, as I did at everyone who came near me. I did not recognize my own mother. She was led away sobbing by the police and I was put in a drunk tank. The next day, there was a court proceeding, which is still foggy in my mind because for the most part I was in a complete blackout. People seemed to float around the room like ghosts; someone in a black robe sat at the front of the room, and a woman sat there weeping. I remember a long ride in the back of a police car with two other shackled prisoners.

The road to this hell had been long and rocky. From a loving wife, mother, busi-

---

FROM "FIFTY YEARS OF GRATITUDE"
June 1994

I first learned about AA in Ohio in August 1938. I had several relapses until my first day of lasting sobriety—Armistice Day, November 11, 1944. I'm very grateful for all that I've achieved in AA: recovery, sobriety, contentment, and the opportunity to share all that I was so generously given. But I will always remember those helpless and hopeless drinking times and early treatment procedures: undergoing the aversion cure, being locked up with mental patients, enduring iced sheets and other shock treatments, withstanding physical beatings in a jail bullpen and an Army guardhouse. And I remember the anguish in the faces of loved ones when it seemed that their prayers for my recovery had failed. Then there was that glorious first memory of freedom, the rapture of not needing the crutch of alcohol—the especial joys of self-forgiveness, the regeneration of hope, and the rebirth of faith. There was the bonus of self-respect, of forgiving and liking oneself as a whole person, in a whole family and a whole community.

George S.

ness woman, licensed airplane pilot, and avid golfer, active in church, as well as business and social affairs, I became a falling-down lush, traveling all over the country in search of fun, men, and adventure. I went from one job to another, from one man to another, from one drunk tank to another, descending in three years from respectable citizen to drunken bum, living on skid row, homeless, defenseless, and completely derelict.

The last job I had was shoveling manure onto a truck and hauling it from local farms to the winery on the island where I worked. My bed was in the basement with rats crawling freely around, my only food scraps the winery owner's maid would bring down to me, which I shared with the rats. A bottle of wine put me to sleep.

One day I decided to die, for I had nothing to live for. My beloved children had been taken away from me by the court, and I could not and would not get sober because reality was too awful to face. I had tried suicide several times by trying to stop breathing, by swallowing a bottle of aspirin, by trying to drown myself twice— anything that wasn't too painful or bloody. But I kept getting rescued. The last time I jumped off a ferry boat with a suitcase loaded with rocks. The suitcase sank, but I didn't, as I had forgotten to attach it to me. The next day, I was committed to the state insane asylum. My first memory of that place was lying on a table surrounded by people dressed in white trying to put wires on me. I fought so hard to keep those wires from touching me that I had to be strapped tightly to the table. I had tried many times to commit suicide, but I didn't want to be electrocuted. Unfortunately, I was only one obese female and unable to stop them from giving me shock treatments. After several months of shock, I began regressing into a catatonic world where nothing could touch me. In a last ditch effort to bring me back from the oblivion I sought, a psychiatrist made me go to an AA meeting. She took all my tranquilizers away, so I would know what was going on. Then, because without tranquilizers I was unpredictable, she put me in a straitjacket, and had an attendant wheel me into the meeting.

At my very first AA meeting there in the hospital, I heard words of love, understanding and compassion, and stories told by beautifully dressed women, parts of which I could identify with, although none of them had fallen off a manure truck and been thrown in Lake Erie to wash off manure and blood from a cut caused by a rusty nail. I believe the hand of God reached down at that meeting and healed me. For from that day thirty-eight years ago to this, I have not had a desire to drink or escape from reality again.

Today I live a busy, productive life, working a full-time night job in a large law firm. I use my computer talents to make a very good living, which allows me to travel all over the world and share my experience, strength, and hope with AA members in Athens, London, Paris, Amsterdam, Munich, and Nassau. I love to tell my story and have an audience of alcoholics laugh with me, cry with me, and hopefully get hope from my story, seeing that if I can come back to sobriety and respectability after my life as a drunk, they can, too. I especially love to tell my story to prisoners and mental patients who identify with me because they too have lost their freedom to alcohol.

One of my fondest memories is the night I told my story in Raiford Prison in Florida and had over 200 men incarcerated for heinous crimes laughing so hard they cried and then coming up and hugging me afterward with tears in their eyes, telling me I had given them hope. And oh, the wondrous joy of Christmas reunions with my scattered family and the laughter and love that is there. Best of all is the peace I have found knowing that I made amends to my mother for all the sorrow I caused her. A few months before she died, I took her to Hawaii for her birthday. It was a gift for both of us.

Pauline B.
Royal Palm Beach, Florida

The Perfect Curve
November 2004

WHEN I WAS fourteen years old, my dad and I were walking down a country road in Indiana when I spotted an empty bottle, curved so it could fit snugly against you in your back pocket. That bottle spoke to me. From then on, I looked for curved bottles. Soon I found one and drank it. It didn't take long for me to become a daily drinker. In those days, alcohol was hard to get, but I found a place where I could get a half-pint for fifty cents.

By the time I got married in 1935, alcohol had become the main object of my life. My wife, DeDe, said she could tell how drunk I was by the way my foot hit the first front step. In addition, my father-in-law owned a drug store and if I told him I had a pain in my stomach, he would dole out the paregoric, which was an opium derivative.

I would lie about how much money I spent. Then I'd feel guilty for wasting money and lying, so I drank to assuage the guilt. (Later in AA, I found out through the Steps about this cycle: drinking, lying, guilt, followed by more drinking, lying, guilt.)

When World War II broke out, I tried to enlist because it sounded like a great opportunity to drink (I'd heard about the weekend adventures of soldiers), but I was rejected because of a chest problem. I ended up going to work in a war plant that manufactured uniforms. It didn't take me long to learn I could trade uniforms for cash, which I spent on booze. Then I made more drinking money from passing out custom uniforms for police and firemen. The plant kept me employed for several years, but I developed a desire for a change of scenery (commonly known in our AA program as a geographical cure).

I went to Chicago with a friend, and between us we worked three jobs. Eventually I was fortunate enough to get on with the phone company as a parts delivery man. The fellow who worked across from me in the supply area also worked nights in a gambling house in Cicero, Illinois, and he got me a job there, primarily because I owned a suit. The casino worked me as a "shill" who attracted men to gambling by betting at the craps tables and carrying on in a loud voice about how much I'd won and what good luck I'd had. I could have all I wanted to drink as long as I didn't get drunk—a dream come true if you're the kind of drunk I was. I held on for about a year before I got fired for—you guessed it—being drunk.

The war was ending, and I opened my own dry-cleaning business in Indianapolis, where I had grown up. My drinking progressed to the point that my wife had to call her girlfriend's brother, who was a doctor, to give me shots of morphine to calm me down. He said I couldn't keep drinking. I saw a psychiatrist who never came right out and said I was alcoholic, but he did say, "Apparently, you are one of those people who just can't drink."

Everyone around me said, "Quit drinking," but no one was able to tell me how. I had an old friend in Florida who was a doctor, and I decided to travel there to see him about my problem. My wife insisted on coming with me. To this day, I don't know how we got the money, but we found a little place to stay and I visited with my friend who said, "Gerald, I can operate on a brain tumor and be successful, but as far as helping a man with his drinking problem, I don't know any way to be successful. You just have to quit drinking." So I did, for two months.

We came back to Indiana, and I still couldn't understand why some people couldn't drink. I was bitter at the doctor, my wife, everyone! But during this time, I began to wonder why I couldn't drink. What was the reason? My grandfather and cousins all drank—maybe it was their fault?

Then the psychiatrist I'd seen called me and asked if I'd go to a place called AA up in Chicago. So that's how I got to my first meeting on November 4, 1947. I haven't had a drink since.

It's hard to explain the feeling I had. I guess the best way is to say I felt like I was home. I walked into that meeting room and a man put out his hand and said, "My name is Clem. Do you have a problem with alcohol? If so, don't drink tonight and come back tomorrow."

I'm grateful for anonymity, because later I found out that this man was a well-known writer for the Chicago Tribune. Had I known who he was when he stuck his hand out and said, "Keep coming back," I probably would have felt as if I didn't belong with such a high-falutin' crowd!

I returned to Indiana, where a friend and I started an AA group with just three

---

FROM "GETTING STUPID"

January 1996

Eventually I lost everything. I was in Orange, Texas, living in a junkyard in the back of what we referred to as the Chevrolet Motel. A friend of mine and I shared this Chevy with a dog, but it got so bad even the dog left. On a cold night in February, we were broke and we were hungry, and my friend said, "I know where we can get a cup of coffee and a sandwich for nothing." We'd been panhandling all day and hadn't made out too well. So we went to this meeting at a church down the road. I was having coffee and a sandwich when a guy came up to me and said, "Are you having a problem with alcohol?" "No," I said, "I'm having a problem without it." That was February 2, 1963, and I've been sober ever since.

I had a great sponsor. I asked him, "What do I have to do to stay sober?" He said, "Get stupid, throw out all your old concepts." He told me to sit down, shut up, and learn to listen, that I had nothing to share but a drunkalog. He was deeply into the Steps, though Step and Big Book meetings weren't around then. I followed that same path and in time I found a whole new way of life.

Phil L.

Malden, Massachusetts

people. We met every day and discussed what was said in those Chicago meetings. Over time we met others and the whole time we talked AA and the Twelve Steps.

It's now 2004 and I'm eighty-nine years old. I live in a retirement home with my wife near Austin, Texas. My doctor here found out I'm a member of AA and said to me, "You keep going to AA. Take every Sunday off from here and go to your meeting. They need you!" My life has been a pleasure to live because of AA and the many wonderful people in it.

Gerald R. (as told to Carolyn C.)
Austin, Texas

A Real War Story
April 2002

I JOINED THE Navy in 1943, and that's when the drinking started. Right after boot camp, I was sent to a service school and was allowed liberty. The Navy still had hammocks then, and after a night of learning to drink beer, it was very difficult to stay in the hammock. After service school, I reported to an LST and participated in the invasion of France, and after the invasion was sent back to Omaha Beach. There wasn't any drinking on the beach except for the bottle of scotch I had taken with me prior to the invasion.

Then I was assigned to the staff for the boat units that were formed for taking the army across the Rhine River. I traveled from unit to unit as they advanced with the army through France, Holland, Belgium, and Germany, and found a wide variety of booze was available. I made my acquaintance with cognac and calvados. There was a song popular at the time that began "Mares eat oats, and does eat oats, and little lambs eat ivy"; our version was "Mares eat oats and calvados and headaches in the morning."

Drinking got me into various situations during the war that could have been serious, but I always seemed to get away without any disciplinary action. One occurred during the Battle of the Bulge when we were in Liege and had just come back from the front. My buddy and I were out after curfew, drinking, wearing our normal uniforms, which consisted of army khakis and a navy foul-weather jacket. We were locked up for the night after we told some MPs that we were filling submarines with helium and flying them up to the Rhine River and were on our way back for another one. We were released in the morning to the officer-in-charge, and when we got back to headquarters, the admiral's yeoman said, "We received a report listing several charges against you and recommending that you be court martialed." But he added, "The admiral hasn't seen this, and mail gets lost during the war, so keep the report as a souvenir. But behave yourselves on the next trip."

That was the pattern during my whole naval career. There were many things I could have gotten punished for, but somehow I always got away with them. In fact, I received five good conduct medals. But this wasn't the case back home. The drinking got worse from year to year until my wife left me to go home to her mother. Then one morning, in the spring of 1959, being unable to function aboard ship, I tried to commit suicide by drinking what I thought was a potent poison. I also put on a Broadway show while doing it, and the Navy sent me to a psychiatric ward. The only thing I learned from that was to never drink poison again, as I hated the process of having my stomach pumped. I spent the next three months in the Navy psychiatric ward. At that time, the Navy didn't have alcoholic treatment centers.

Then the miracle began to happen. I was put back on active duty and transferred from the hospital to the admiral's staff in Pearl Harbor, Hawaii, in August 1959. This is not how the Navy usually fills vacancies on an admiral's staff, but I think my Higher Power stepped in and started leading me out of the alcoholic life, as I seemed incapable of doing it on my own. Soon after, that my wife, who with our five children was living in Connecticut, went to bed one night totally depressed with her lot in life. Her brother, an Air Force pilot who'd been killed in a plane crash in 1954, appeared to her in a dream and said she would be in Hawaii on the 24th of November. She awoke the next morning full of hope and peace and, against the advice of her family, doctor, and priest, made arrangements to come to Hawaii. She and our five children sailed on an Army transport, arriving in Hawaii on November 24.

I went back to AA. I had previously gone to a few meetings in Boston in 1957, but when the ship left the Boston area, I started to drink again. In Hawaii, I met a wonderful group of people at what was then the Hickam Group. My sponsor called me every morning and made arrangements to pick me up that evening to go to a meeting. The women in the group gave my wife a tremendous amount of help and love at the same time. AA became the most important thing in our lives. My home group met on Wednesday and Saturday nights, and except for the rare time when I was on duty one of those nights, nothing was ever scheduled to interfere with the meetings. Most meetings were open, and my wife went to them with me four or five times a week. She also got involved with the new Al-Anon group that was getting started. There weren't that many AA meetings in Hawaii at that time, and probably about 100 or so people in AA, but it was great traveling to different parts of Oahu during the week to catch a meeting, especially taking part in the discussions on the ride to the meeting and on the way home. Besides going to meetings, five or six of us would meet once a week, alternating homes to read a chapter of the Big Book or the "Twelve and Twelve," and spend a couple of hours discussing it. There was no time limit on these informal get-togethers.

Then one night at a meeting, I experienced the biggest thing that ever happened: the light came on inside my brain and I realized that I was an alcoholic and just couldn't drink. After that, I no longer thought of a drink—or of the waterfront bars in foreign ports with the dim lights, music, and excitement—as being attractive. Instead, I knew that a drink would lead to a drunk with the usual consequences: with me broke, looking for a place to sober up, and trying to get out of trouble. The acceptance of being an alcoholic and knowing without a doubt that I couldn't drink were the starting points of enjoying sobriety.

One day, I was complaining to my sponsor about some problem in my life and he said, "Things are bad, but bad in relationship to what?" That statement has stayed with me all these years. When I have a problem or situation in my life, I remember that statement. Nothing that has happened to me over the past forty-one years is as bad as the day the Navy put me in a locked and padded cell, took away my belt, shoestrings, and razor, and assigned personnel to look through the peephole in the cell door every ten minutes.

In the summer of 1963, after four years of sobriety, I was transferred to the Washington, D. C., area. The first thing I did was find a home group that met on Wednesday and Saturday nights. I stayed real active in AA for several years, attending several other meetings a week, and sponsoring newcomers. I also was able to give a talk about AA to the psychologists at the local Army hospital, and it was the seed planted for the start of an AA group there.

After forty-one years of sobriety in AA, life and my involvement with AA have slowed down quite a bit. I still go to two meetings a week, one at the local mental health center which is only a mile from the house; I enjoy walking over there on Tuesday evenings. I have eternal gratitude for Alcoholics Anonymous for the years of sobriety, peace, serenity, and joy of living that I have been able to experience.

When I first started in AA, I began each day asking God to help keep me sober that day, and ended each night by thanking him for another day of sobriety. I still end each day that way, as I have done almost every night during the past forty-one years. It is a routine for me, but every once in a while I pause to reflect on what it really means. I do it every night so that God won't change his mind, as I truly believe he helped lead me from the pits of alcoholism to the AA way of life.

Bill H.

Alexandria, Virginia

—∿∿—

From Rags to Riches
January 2005

AT FORTY YEARS old, lying on the floor alone and hung over, I realized that the party was over. It had begun back when I joined the celebration of the end of World War II. After years of our servicemen and women being away, we lifted our glasses to their safe homecoming. But when most people had put their glasses down, mine was still high in the air. I loved dressing up, going to parties, clowning around, and dancing. The excitement never stopped.

As the party continued, my life grew emptier. I stuck to the ease of socializing that drinking alcohol gave me. However, as much as alcohol was giving me friends and good times, it also took away much in my life. It took away babies, first and second husbands, health, an eye and part of another eye. It took away friends as well, although I could always make new friends—drinking friends.

Prayers took the form of "gimmee": Give me a better job, a better husband, more money. Thanking God for what I actually had never entered my mind. An unfulfilled, vacant feeling remained that led me to a bottle of gin every day. When this led to sadness, my intelligence told me to switch to scotch, then to black rum, straight alcohol, and, at times, all mixed in one big drink. Sometimes, for a few hours, the drinking would help me overcome my utter loneliness. But inevitably, the loneliness would return, along with guilt.

By the 1960s, I was ready to change my life. Unfortunately, AA was not well-publicized in Montreal at that time. I didn't know where to go.

The world around me seemed to have turned black. My heart was heavy and my soul lost. People left me alone because I was unpredictable. I became depressed. I would invariably ask myself, How do I get out of this mess? I would then think, I've gone nowhere, done nothing. What I've done hasn't worked. God doesn't love me the way he loves other people.

At forty years old, I didn't know who I was and I didn't know what I felt. The year was 1966, and I spent most nights passed out on the floor of the basement room I had rented. After a particularly long session of boozing, limp and unable to go to work, I thought I was having DTs. A vision appeared as a moving picture over my entire living space. A woman in rags, bent over and worn out, begging with a cup, was sitting on the corner of Peel and St. Catherine Streets. Although hundreds of people were walking by, she was alone on that street. Nobody wanted to look at her. They turned their heads away. I don't know what you'd call this picture, but I call it my spiritual experience.

The vision stayed with me for what seemed like twenty-four hours. I sensed that the woman in rags was me. The cup for money was the big thing in the picture. I knew that the money was for booze. I couldn't breathe without drinking. Booze made me what I was.

Stunned by the clarity of this vision, I became instantly relieved, and I happily told myself that from this day onward I would never take another drink. I was not at all worried about how this was going to occur and, having no fear of any kind, the image of a new life unfolded before me. With this vision in mind, I proceeded to detox myself alone, a very dangerous procedure that could have caused a heart attack. For three days and three nights, I drank water, smoked cigarettes, sat at my kitchen table, and played solitaire. Well, I can't say that I sat. I couldn't stay in one position for long. I couldn't sleep because I couldn't lie down.

The next day, fear set in. I thought, I'd better get out of here. Someone will bring me booze and I'll want to drink. I decided to call an old friend who had deserted me during the past year when I drank constantly and was unpredictable, peeing in plants, removing my glass eye and placing it in drinks, stealing food, and sleeping in her bathtub. By the grace of God she was home, and after much pleading on my part, she agreed to let me come to her home. She laid down some rules: I was to take a cab, I could not buy a bottle on the way, I could not swear, and I could not remove my eye.

When I got to her home, I found out that she had been in AA for a year. She was with two friends and they were all going to a meeting on the Kahnawake reservation.

At the meeting, I learned that I had an incurable disease and that the only way out was to surrender my entire life to a God of my understanding. They told me I could be a member by saying so—that's all. I heard that I could recover from twenty-three years of daily drinking by becoming completely honest and that insanity would disappear if I asked God to take it away.

Those people were smart. They didn't give me a Big Book or folders of literature. They gave me what I consider the single most important piece of literature: a meeting list. From then on I have always carried a meeting list and a quarter for a phone call because I don't know when I am going to want another drink. I need a program of recovery. I'm crazy.

Look at what God did for me in 1966: I had no winter coat, no hat, no boots and one simple, black dress. The first month of my new life, I walked into a store and bought a three-piece ensemble: a coral sweater, a coral and white skirt, and a coral and white topcoat. The whole outfit was extremely fashionable and it cost me a total of $35. The memory lingers today, the excitement and gratitude of living in the real world with store clerks, cash on hand, and cash left over to buy food. No more filling up my handbag with food from the happy hour at bars.

In the early years of recovery, the word "soul" still left a blank. I was undecided on whether or not I had a soul. It seemed lost in an uncaring, unloving, and self-centered existence. My soul remained a mystery until my Higher Power settled inside me, appearing to me as a very real feeling of love and caring. Kindness slowly took precedence, and I became comfortable with the idea that I didn't need a drink.

I am convinced that alcohol destroys us from the inside out: It so fills us with guilt and fear that no other feelings can be felt, not even the feeling of our souls.

Before recovery, I was mortified at the thought that people might discover I was not the self-assured woman I made myself out to be. If they knew about my weaknesses, they would have more reason to avoid me. Getting a sponsor drastically changed the necessity of maintaining this fragile self-image. Through uncovering and admitting my character defects, I realized that I was no different than the people I was so afraid of. I understood that we were all suffering and that I didn't need to disguise my authentic self. Having an honest relationship with my sponsor allowed me an honest relationship with myself and others.

Growing up into a spiritually mature adult has been difficult at times. It has taught me that I will surely be able to grow into the person God wants me to be if I don't take a drink. After a long time, I finally realized that I cannot totally rely on anybody except God. At the same time, I understand that I need the Fellowship.

Attending meetings, I have been forced to find ways to change my behavior. For example, in my first years I was so sneaky and secretive that everything backfired. At a meeting, a member suggested that I write instead of thinking, and to share everything with the group. I didn't know this was possible. I did it and the process made me authentic. It showed me how ridiculous I could be when I was on my own. I learned that if I had the capacity to be honest, I would get better.

Serenity and peace of mind are a direct result of accepting our lives as they are at this moment, and all the money in the world cannot purchase this kind of peace.

Eileen P.

Cornwall, Ontario

Living History

> "... he was the first living human with whom I had ever talked,
> who knew what he was talking about in regard to alcoholism
> from actual experience. In other words, he talked my language.
> He knew all the answers, and certainly not because he had
> picked them up in his reading."

"Dr. Bob's Nightmare," Alcoholics Anonymous

AA's early years were exciting, often turbulent times. An AA member was considered a longtimer if he had one or two years, newcomers often went out and drank again, Twelfth-Step calls on active drunks were common, there were far fewer meetings than at present, and the Traditions were still evolving. There were many struggles, some failures, and growing success in this period of trial and error. When Bill W. first wrote about the Ninth Tradition (in the August 1948 issue of Grapevine), saying, "Each AA Group needs the least possible organization," a few old-timers must have chuckled, "Why, AA never has been organized!"

Through the first-hand accounts that follow, we can begin to see the creative chaos out of which AA grew—what Bill W. called the "benign anarchy" of the Fellowship before it grew into a democracy. What sustained early members then was a simple but profound hunger to stay sober and adopt this new way of life. We are here because of them, because of the power of one alcoholic communicating with another.

—∿∿—

Sober for Thirty Years
May 1968

AS I NOTED in my story, "The Vicious Cycle," in the Big Book, I came into the Fellowship in New York in January 1938. At that time, it was just leaving the Oxford Group. There was one closed discussion meeting a week, at Bill's home in Brooklyn—attendance, six or eight men, with only three members who had been sober more than one year: Bill, Hank, and Fitz. This is about all that had been accomplished in the four years with the New York Oxford Group.

During those early meetings at Bill's, they were flying blind, with no creed or procedure to guide them, though they did use quite a few of the Oxford sayings and the Oxford Absolutes. Since both Bill and Dr. Bob had almost-overnight religious experiences, it was taken for granted that all who followed their way would have the same sort of experience. So the early meetings were quite religious, in both New York and Akron. There was always a Bible on hand, and the concept of God was all biblical.

Into this fairly peaceful picture came I, their first self-proclaimed atheist, completely against all religions and conventions. I was the captain of my own ship. (The only trouble was, my ship was completely disabled and rudderless.) So naturally I started fighting nearly all the things Bill and the others stood for, especially religion, "the God bit." But I did want to stay sober, and I did love the understanding fellowship. So I became quite a problem to that early group, with my constant haranguing against all the spiritual angles.

All of a sudden, the group became really worried. Here I had stayed sober five whole months while fighting everything the others stood for. I was now number four in "seniority." I found out later they had a prayer meeting on "what to do with Jim." The consensus seemed to have been that they hoped I would either leave town or get drunk.

That prayer must have been right on target, for I was suddenly taken drunk on a sales trip. This became the shock and the bottom I needed. At this time, I was selling auto polish to jobbers for a company that Bill and Hank were sponsoring, and I was doing pretty well, too. But despite this, I was tired and completely isolated there in Boston. My fellow alcoholics really put the pressure on as I sobered up after four days of no relief. For the first time, I admitted I couldn't stay sober alone. My closed mind opened a bit. Those folks back in New York, the folks who believed, had stayed sober. And I hadn't. Since this episode, I don't think I have ever argued with anyone else's beliefs. Who am I to say?

I finally crawled back to New York and was soon back in the fold. About this time, Bill and Hank were just beginning to write the AA Big Book. I do feel sure my experience was not in vain, for "God" was broadened to cover all types and creeds: "God as we understood Him."

I feel my spiritual growth over these past thirty years has been very gradual and steady. I have no desire to "graduate" from AA. I try to keep my memories green by staying active in AA—a couple of meetings weekly.

For the new agnostic or atheist just coming in, I will try to give very briefly my milestones in recovery:

1. The first power I found greater than myself was John Barleycorn.
2. The AA Fellowship became my Higher Power for the first two years.
3. Gradually, I came to believe that God and good were synonymous and were to be found in all of us.
4. And I found that by meditating and trying to tune in on my better self for guidance and answers, I became more comfortable and steady.

J. B.

San Diego, California

⸎

The Seven-Day Test
November 2001

IN 1945, IN Miami, Florida, I met a woman from New York who'd been a waitress at Child's Restaurant. A group of AA members often came in and sat at her table after a meeting, and one of these, Jack C., was now in Miami, and she introduced us. He told me he was an alcoholic and a member of AA and was soon to celebrate his first-year birthday. I had heard of the organization vaguely. Someone had mentioned a magazine article and I was curious. He invited us to his anniversary meeting, where he was the speaker.

We went up a flight of steps in a building near downtown Miami. A man was standing at the top of the stairs greeting everyone. When he took my hand, he asked, "Are you one of us?" I replied, "Well, potentially, I guess." He asked if I lived in Miami, and I told him I'd just moved there. He said, "Great! Go to all the bars and clubs, live it up, and maybe you'll make it." I thought: A bunch of nuts.

It was an open speaker meeting with remarks later. It was an interesting talk, but what surprised me was that several women got up and said, "I'm an alcoholic." How degrading!

They gave me a card with the Twelve Steps on one side and the Serenity Prayer on the other. I read the Steps and thought, I might as well join a convent.

I tore the card up and went about taking the advice of the greeter at the top of the stairs. But I never forgot that meeting.

Four years later, in 1949, I was in South Bend, Indiana. I was in a bad marriage, drinking constantly, and I found AA's number in the telephone book. Someone came to see me, loaned me the Big Book, and took me to a meeting. It was in a man's home and there were seven or eight present. One man looked at me and said, "You're not ready for this—you're too young and look too good." Another said, "You probably have two more years' drinking in you." I had no place else to go so I stayed.

At that time, newcomers were required to attend a meeting once a week in a home where a man explained the Steps. The first meeting was on Step One and the host said, "If you have any doubts, there is a test you can take. Take one drink only on Monday, two only on Tuesday, three on Wednesday, four on Thursday, and five on Friday. On Saturday and Sunday take none, and if you can do that, the chances are pretty good that you are not alcoholic." I knew I couldn't do it.

They had a club that you were allowed to join after one month's sobriety. I hung out there and absorbed a lot of AA from members. Everyone was reading *Power Through Constructive Thinking* by Emmet Fox. I bought a copy, and it changed my life.

I gave up on the marriage and went to work for a company in Chicago. I went to meetings every night. The first one was in Bennie's Basement and as far as I know that was the name of the group. I found a great sponsor named Mary, whose last name I can't remember today. There was a Sunday breakfast meeting at one of the hotels and a speaker meeting on Tuesday night at a building on Randolph Street. One night a buzz went through the room: "Bill just came in." They called him to the podium, and he thanked us for being there. I loved AA in Chicago. It was my whole life. I miss the old days.

I particularly remember a man named Fairfax T., who told me he had been in AA for ten years. I was impressed. I later learned he'd been attending meetings that long but had not stopped drinking. Nevertheless, he helped me. Later I heard that some of the men were so disgusted that they held him down and poured whiskey down his throat.

In a few months, my company sent me to Kalamazoo, Michigan, where I had trouble finding AA. Finally I was directed by the police department. The meeting was on a side street, up a flight of stairs. There were some men playing cards in the back of the room. I asked, "Is this AA?" One man said, "Yes, but we ain't got no women." I said, "You do now," and sat down on a couch in the front of the room. Shortly a nice-looking, well-dressed man came in and greeted me. He explained that at one time they had a girl but she didn't come anymore. He made me welcome.

I continued to go to meetings there, but then the wives learned there was "a woman" up there. The group decided to open the meeting so the wives could come. Shortly afterward, my anonymity was broken, and when my landlady learned I was an alcoholic, she was quite upset.

After a few months, the company sent me to a small town—Alliance, Ohio. No other women attended AA in the Alliance group. I was invited to a home on Saturday night. The men played poker in the kitchen and I was delegated to the living room with the wives. One looked at me and asked, "Don't you feel a lot better since you quit drinking?" I said, "No." I was miserable and thought, Drinking was never this bad.

I attended the first International Convention in Cleveland in 1950, and

---

An old-timer in the northeast United States didn't like to use the term "pigeons" when referring to the women she sponsored. She much preferred to call them her "babies." One day, while shopping in a mall, she ran into one of her sponsees, who was there with her husband and their new baby. The sponsor looked at the infant and declared, "My goodness, what a beautiful baby!" The husband, suppressing a smile, answered, "Thank you, we prefer to call him our pigeon."

Anonymous, July 2005

heard Dr. Bob's last talk. The Twelve Traditions were accepted later that day. But I was so lonely in Ohio that I made a conscious decision to drink again when I went home on vacation.

Two and a half year later I came back to the Fellowship in Lexington, Kentucky, where I had moved after another marriage. I was ready.

There were only two meetings a week in Lexington. They were both speaker meetings. One of the first questions I was asked was "Do you play poker?" There was none of the spirituality I had experienced in Chicago. It took six years to start a discussion meeting in 1958 at Gratz Park. It caused a split in AA and much resentment, but the group flourished.

I attended the Yale School of Alcohol Studies in 1960 and worked with the state for several years. I was a founding member of the board for a rehabilitation home for addicted women.

I still attend meetings and sponsor a few, but AA is different—more organized, with printed instructions on how to conduct a meeting. It was intimate in the beginning. Now the meetings are large, and I know very few. I'm glad I was around in the early days.

Mary P.
Lexington, Kentucky

—*◦◦◦*—

Practice These Principles
November 1997

WHENEVER I SEE people fleeing from the opportunity to hear a discussion about the Traditions, it gives me pause for thought. I recall some things I witnessed in AA before the Twelve Traditions were accepted at our first International Convention in July 1950. I was part of the discussion our group had about the Traditions, which had been suggested but not yet accepted by the membership as a whole. We were encouraged to talk about them and send back any suggestions or changes we wished to recommend. This was early in April 1950.

Let me share with you some of the ideas that came out of our group from well-meaning members.

Some people in our group thought that only college graduates should be members of AA. (They didn't say you had to bring in your diploma, but I think that would have been next!)

We had groups in areas where there were large numbers of black people. They were listed in our group's list as "interracial groups." That meant anyone was welcome to go there, but most people attending would be black. I was taken aback but gratified the first time I spoke at an interracial group when one of the members called out to me, "Amen, Sister, Amen!" We took a new member who was black to an interracial group so he would know there was such a group. We next brought him to our home group. One of our ladies took us aside and said, "Don't bring him around here!"

Talk about taken aback! She sweetly explained that some of our membership had servants; she said, "And you know how people talk!"

We had never had a woman as a chair of our group. One of the male members

---

FROM "CELEBRATING OUR BEGINNING"

June 1982

Never shall I forget my first Founders' Day event in Akron, birthplace of AA. It was held in the Mayflower Hotel dining room. The date: June 10, 1945. I had been sober only three months. During my last binge, the country had changed presidents, and I did not know it till my third day in the St. Thomas alcoholic ward, where they showed me a newspaper.

I spent six days in the ward, and there I had the opportunity to meet Sister Ignatia and the beloved Dr. Bob, co-founder of AA. Dr. Bob was on the staff of the hospital. He would come in to see us twice a day. There were eight of us.

Most of the early members who came to our bedsides have gone to their reward. I was only thirty-four at the time. Dr. Bob and the other AAs took much time with me. Today, I am humbly grateful for the message of hope that was passed on to me. I shall always have a place in my heart and mind for the six days I spent there. It was there my real adult life began.

D. K.

Sun City Center, Florida

used to stand up and say, "When a man comes through that door, he needs to see a man standing up there!" I can't recall who was the first woman chairperson, but it wasn't me.

A certain faction was attempting to keep women from becoming members of their group because they said, and I quote, "They will cause trouble among the men."

When the first two unmarried members planned to live together, one of the women members proclaimed, "Membership in AA is by attraction rather than promotion, and that isn't very attractive, is it?" I think she wanted to throw them out of the group there and then. Thank God for the Traditions!

Concerning group conscience: our group met in a hospital where the staff representing the hospital was adamantly against accepting any money from us, even when we had explained about how we needed to be self-supporting. (It may have had something to do with their tax base.) Before it had been resolved, the whole group was in an uproar.

We were able to agree to discuss the entire matter with representatives from the New York office. We invited them to send speakers to our meeting on a certain date and they did. When we had listened to their suggestions about how the problem could best be handled, we prepared to vote our group conscience.

Lo and behold, we looked up and there was a whole bunch of AAs who were not members of our group, who were signing up new people so they could vote as part of the group conscience. Upon further reflection, we agreed that to vote as part of a group conscience, it was necessary to be a member of the group and not just someone who was rounded up at the last minute to carry the day for their way.

There is one other example I'd like to give about the group conscience and of how helpful it can be in time of trouble. We recently had a secretary in our group who no longer wanted to fill his position. He said if we didn't replace him he would close the group. That was so patently outrageous that I just ignored him!

He had invited me to speak at our meeting and I had agreed to do it. I had invited another woman to speak with me. Then my phone rang and it was the secretary. He told me I needn't bother to come to speak as he had canceled the meeting. I was stunned and blurted out, "You can't do that!" He assured me that he could and would.

I told him Jen and I would be there to speak at 7:30 and if anyone was there, we would speak to them. If no one was there, we would speak to each other. I told him if no one was willing to be secretary, I would act as one until they could find someone else.

He warned me against getting involved; he said the money from the treasury could not be accounted for and I might be blamed for taking it. I told him it was not unheard of in the old days for a treasurer to take the funds and go off on a drunk. I said the group conscience should be consulted about what to do. I am happy to tell you that we did vote the group conscience and the group is "hanging in."

Marie K.

Laguna Hills, California

—◆◇◆—

From Wagon Trains to Jets
June 1995

MY FIRST REAL contact with Alcoholics Anonymous was made in Yonkers, New York, where I grew up. I had an asthmatic sister in the hospital; she told me that she was dying and she wanted me to raise her eight children.

We had two other sisters, but for some reason she wanted me to raise these kids. "There's only one thing, Nancy," she said. "You're going to have to stop drinking." "Katharine," I said, "you'll just have to stay alive because I will never stop drinking. Furthermore, if I had never taken a drink in my life and was confronted with raising eight kids—I'd start!" She began to laugh, and she laughed so hard she coughed up all the congestion, and her lungs cleared up, and she left the hospital. All the nuns (it was a Catholic hospital) were saying, "It's a miracle." "No," I said, "it was me."

I knew I had a drinking problem; I knew drinking in bed wasn't social drinking. But I had an image to maintain. I was a decorator; I had to look good. I put a lot of money into clothes, beauty shops, and massages. I had to look rich and that was some job. I haven't worked so hard since. My husband belonged to three golf courses, I belonged to three bars, and I never let his golf interfere with my drinking. I had terrible hangovers but I'd take care of them with the hair of the dog that bit me. I kept a stash of booze in a roasting pan in the kitchen. I made sure I always had a backup.

I couldn't stop drinking and I knew it; I also knew that I'd drink for the rest of my life. I loved to drink. I only felt normal when I drank; when I wasn't drinking, I felt very, very weird. When I came into AA, they asked me if I took a morning drink. "No," I said, "I don't get up in the morning. But I take a drink as soon as I get up."

My sister Katharine tried everything to get me sober. One day she came to my house with a chocolate cake; a doctor had told her that what alcoholics really wanted was sugar, not booze. So there I was in bed, about halfway through a bottle, and I couldn't wait to get rid of Katharine and she knew it. "If you'll eat a piece of this cake," she said, "I'll leave you to your drinking." "I can't eat the cake," I said, "but give me the Manhattan telephone directory—there's an outfit in New York called Alcoholics Anonymous that has a bead on this drinking thing. I'll call them and see what they do." Then Katharine told me that her husband's best friend was an AA member, and she asked me if I'd like to see him. I said yes just to get her out of the room.

I don't know how it happened, but I didn't finish that bottle, and somehow I got up, got dressed, and waited for Mr. AA. He didn't show then and he didn't show the next day. On the third day, I called my sister and said, "Where is this genius who's going to stop my drinking?" She said, "He and his fellow members are discussing whether or not you qualify for AA." I had a short fuse, and I was incensed that anyone would think I wasn't eligible for AA. Later, the man's ten-year-old son came over with the Big Book in a brown paper bag; he shoved it at me and ran. I liked children, and I was disturbed that he was so scared of me.

I read the book from cover to cover; I couldn't put it down. I saw myself on every page. And the stories: I could see that the way they drank was the way I drank. I could see that it had gone bad on them and I knew it had gone bad on me too. I put the book in the fireplace behind the logs—it was summertime—because I didn't want anyone in the house to read it and decide I ought to join. I didn't want to join. I had looked at the Twelve Steps and I didn't think a spiritual way of life was for me.

I continued to drink until the fall of that year. Then one morning I was having a very bad time of it, and I called my brother-in-law's friend, the AA member. "You know," I told him, "I read that entire book. I know all there is to know about alcoholism; I'm very well-informed. So how come I'm still drinking?" He didn't answer my question, but he asked me if I'd like to go to a meeting that night. I said, "I don't know. What's it like?" He said, "Everyone there will be just like you—an alcoholic. You'll feel very comfortable." I asked, "What do they look like?" and he replied, "They look just like you." "Well," I said, "they must be gorgeous!"

I went with him to the meeting. There weren't any women. This was 1944 and there were maybe a total of three or four women in New York, and that was it. There were six men at this meeting—three lawyers, a butcher, a cop, and a guy who worked in a malt factory who said he couldn't stay sober because the malt went into his pores. That was solved easily enough—we got him another job. I loved it; they were wonderful men. I decided that they were far too wonderful to have to stay sober. "Give me three months," I told them, "and I'll get us all out of this." I thought that if we had all crossed over this invisible line, I could find that line and we could all cross back again! They knew I was an alcoholic and they just let me go about my business.

TAKING IT ON THE ROAD

I decided to do some research, to interview AA members. There weren't many meetings in those days; you had to travel. I covered a radius of about 100 miles, which included Manhattan, Long Island, Westchester County, Albany, and parts of New Jersey and Connecticut. I'd go to meetings, listen to the stories, pick the best one, and interview that person. This was hard work and I was plenty thirsty—it was nuts. In about three months, I came to the conclusion that:

1.   It was the first drink that activated the obsession—if
      I took that first drink, I was gone.
2.   Alcoholism is progressive—once an alcoholic,
      always an alcoholic.

I talked it over with the membership. I told them yes, I knew I would have to quit, but I was only thirty-one and I wanted to wait until I was in my forties. They didn't tell me no. They told me to put my car up on blocks—don't drive. A fellow who happened to be a guard at a womens' hospital told me that if I landed in jail, he knew someone who could get me out. Meanwhile, this thing kept hammering in my brain: "What are you waiting for? What are you waiting for?"

Suddenly I decided it would be a good idea if I became a member of AA. I wrote an acceptance note, like you would do for a wedding invitation: "Nancy O. accepts with pleasure the kind invitation of Alcoholics Anonymous to become a member." Along with the acceptance, I put a clean piece of paper that would be a letter of resignation if I slipped (everyone in those days talked about slips because a lot of us were slipping).

Nobody ever gave me a hard time, nobody tried to reform me. How smart can you get? They knew how it was with me because they knew how it was with themselves. It was love. And all of sudden—sober now—there was this tug at my heart, the love of one alcoholic for another.

"I'LL REMEMBER YOU FOR THE REST OF MY LIFE"

At three months I had to speak—everybody did. I had to go over to Jersey. I was sick and nervous, throwing up all day, and I called Lois K., my sponsor, and asked, "Why is this good for alcoholics?" She said, "You're thinking about impressing them tonight—that's not the purpose. The purpose is to help one other person in the room, if you can." When I spoke that night, I told the group what my sponsor had said and how nervous I felt. After the meeting, a blind woman came up and asked me, "May I feel your face?" She touched my face and she said, "I knew you looked like that. I'll remember you for the rest of my life." I went home and cried for an hour and a half, to think that I could help someone who was blind and in an alcoholic mess. For the first time in my life, I realized I had done something worthwhile. That was my first taste of humility.

WORKING WITH OTHERS

When I was new, I was the only woman around, so team leaders would call me up to be on their team to speak with them. My family was having fits because I was doing this, and finally they said to me, "Nobody has ever disgraced us like this." I said, "No, we all died, and I want to live." One person said to me, "It's like wearing a sign on your back, Nancy." Well, I took exception to that, so I went out and bought a fire-engine-red dress. Whenever I spoke, I'd say, "The reason I'm wearing this red dress is because there might be a woman around, and I don't want her to miss me in the crowd. I just want her to know I'm here, I'm for her, and I'm with her."

Lois K. had been sober for four years when she became my sponsor. She lived in White Plains, and I lived in Yonkers; I asked her if I could call her and that started the relationship. We were in touch every day, and we did a lot of Twelfth Step work together, helping women in Westchester County, and it was hard. The first womens' meeting was at my house. It was Lois who came up with the idea for the Grapevine. Lois was also very involved with her sponsor, Marty M., and the National Council on Alcoholism. I could have been, but I never cared for the idea. I liked working with alcoholics in AA better.

My group was very active working with alcoholics in jails and hospitals and mental hospitals. One day I went to see a woman in the hospital, and on my way out, her psychiatrist asked to speak to me. He told me that his parents had spent thousands of dollars on his education, and the woman I'd just seen wouldn't say two words to him. He wanted to know why he was failing and I was succeeding.

I told him that I had a story and he didn't. He had the education, but I was an alcoholic with a story that she identified with and understood. I talked to the woman, told her to cooperate with the doctor, and maybe she could be helped by him. I did Twelfth Step work with this doctor for five years; we did a lot of good work with alcoholics. I said to him, "Don't ask them why they drink. They don't know. They expect you to know, and you don't know either—nobody does. So don't ask them."

KEEPING IT GREEN

I'd give people the Big Book and tell them to read what I'd underlined because I knew they wouldn't read the whole book at first. I'd underline parts like the jay-walker, the Steps, "no human power," and anything I thought they could identify with. This would prompt them to go on and read the rest of the book, and then they'd call me. It helped me a great deal, and it still helps me. It keeps my sobriety green, it keeps it alive. I'm not one who says, Let the newcomers do it. There's plenty of work for old-timers. I haven't been into jails for a while, but I'm still doing hospital work.

The second woman I ever sponsored was a prostitute. She was always landing in jail, and they would remand her to my custody. I didn't care that she was a prostitute but I did care that she was an alcoholic. One time I called the jail to tell her I'd come and pick her up. "Wait 'til this afternoon," she said, "I'm playing cards with the warden and I have him on the hook for a few dollars." After she got sober and embarked on a spiritual way of life, her life began to change. She got a job, and later she moved to a new place, where nobody knew her, and started a group.

Another gal I went to see in jail greeted me with, "St. Paul was in jail, you know." "Yeah," I said, "but not for burning tents." She was in because she had burned her apartment and been labeled a pyromaniac. I explained to her jailers that she was an alcoholic—possibly a pyromaniac too, but definitely an alcoholic. I'd been to her apartment and taken out a bushel basket full of bottles from underneath her mattress. She was a schoolteacher, a very, very quiet woman. I took her to meetings with me, and then she went back home to start a group of her own. That's how AA grew in those days. That's how we helped each other.

Once a man came over from Bronxville to ask our group to help him start a group there. During the discussion that followed, someone said, "There are too many snobs in Bronxville. Nobody will come to a group there." I said, "I don't see why snobbery should carry the death penalty. I think we should give this man our support." Later on the man thanked me, and when I asked why he was thanking me, he said, "Because I'm a Bronxville snob."

GROWING THROUGH TRIAL AND ERROR

At this time, we called AA a loosely-knit organization. I said, "It's so loosely knit we're all going to fall through!" It wasn't an organization because nobody could organize us. We wouldn't accept any outside contributions because we didn't want anyone telling us what to do. There were no leaders, so we had to figure it out for ourselves, and that was mighty difficult.

There were many differences of opinion, and that's the way the Fellowship grew. Let someone get a resentment and we'd have a new group! For instance, there was a woman who baked a cake every week; we called it a nut cake—good name for it!—but some people didn't think it was a good idea, so we had a controversy over this foolish cake. Those who wanted the cake stayed, and those who didn't left and started another group.

I remember I called my first sponsor one time and exclaimed, "I don't know what I'm doing!" "None of us do," she replied. We used to take alcoholics off stools in bars and bring them to meetings drunk. Finally somebody said, "I don't think we're doing the right thing." And then the publicity problems—alcoholics bragging about how they saved this one and that one. We made a lot of mistakes. On the basis of our mistakes, Bill W. put together the Twelve Traditions. He did it with a whole lot of help from all of us. The early members brought us one Tradition at a time, in the long form—for our group conscience and vote. We discussed each one, took out anything that we didn't want, made amendments, and then voted. I consider the Twelve Traditions to be the foundation of AA. There were a great many other things that contributed to this foundation, but this was the first really progessive step for our Fellowship.

A TWENTY-FOUR-HOUR PROGRAM

When I was about seven years sober, I started doing Twelfth Step work with alcoholics who were in relapse, and I did this exclusively for the next seven years. The first question I would ask someone was, "Were you on the twenty-four-hour program?" I never got a yes. You work differently with relapsers; they've been around AA, they know people, they know open meetings, they know closed meetings, they know names. Sometimes they're well-known because they used to do a lot of Twelfth Step work themselves. When I was living in Westchester, I'd pick people up and take them into Manhattan to one of the big meetings. This was 1951 or later. I'd say, "We're going to sit in the back; never mind the speaker, just look around the room and tell yourself that all these people are getting sober. They don't know me, they've never seen me before in their lives, they're just getting sober the way I am. And if I practice the AA program, I'll get sober too." I would never talk about anything except getting reestablished as a member of AA, that and the twenty-four-hour program—and so I was forced to practice it.

There's probably nothing more important than a home group. I've been going to the same home group since I moved to California, thirteen years ago. I couldn't have gotten sober without a home group. What I like about a home group is this: you never have to make a decision, it's automatic. You know that's where you're going. This is where the Twelfth Step gets fulfilled, in all meetings really, but particularly in the home group. That's where we reach out to newcomers, we greet people. Everything comes out of the home group: invitations to speak, people to sponsor, being active in AA—it all comes out of the home group.

FROM WAGON TRAINS TO JETS

I sometimes get asked if AA has changed since I first encountered it, and I think how, when I came in, people were fascinated by the wagon train feeling of AA—that we were small, and all knew one another, and were close despite our differences. Now it's like the Concorde jet. It's fast. People come in, they get sober or they go out, they get busy with life, they move away, they go to other groups. When I came in, the membership was estimated at 5,000. Today you and I are members of an international Fellowship of more than two million alcoholics. Think about that! When we go to sleep tonight, there will be alcoholics working with each other somewhere in the world. It never stops. That's a long way from 1944, when I came in. One thing will never change, though: I need you just as much as you need me. We need each other—and our Higher Power. That's where the strength is.

Nancy O.
Lafayette, California

———∿∿∿———

It Works for Me
September 2007

MY SOBRIETY DATE is August 15, 1947.

During World War II, I served as a naval aviator flying single-engine seaplanes that were catapulted off cruisers and battleships. The catapult shot didn't cure a hangover, but for a little while it really took your mind off it. In the summer of 1945, I ended up in a Navy hospital with pneumonia, and I went into DTs. I was in the hospital for four weeks. I got drunk nine of my last ten nights there, so obviously I didn't learn a great deal. I got out of the service in December 1945, and continued to drink, gradually coming to the realization that I couldn't handle it, but I didn't know how to stop.

Finally, on a steamy Saturday morning in August 1947, I called the Chicago AA office, which put me in touch with an AA, and I met with him that afternoon. He lived in Oak Park, the Chicago suburb where I lived, and he'd been sober for five years. AA was only twelve years old at the time, so he had been sober nearly half as long as AA had been in existence. I was twenty-five years old.

I was brought up in a traditional Christian religion. Its followers declared that they had the only true way to God. At the time of my entrance into AA, I believed in nothing. Looking back, it seems to me that my problem was not an unwillingness to believe in God; I was simply unable to believe in that concept of God and I didn't know any other way to find him.

That first day, this man talked to me about "God as we understood him." The bewilderment and antagonism of years began to melt, thawed by this unheard-of approach to God. Nobody argued about whose Higher Power was higher.

The next day, he took me to the Sunday morning breakfast AA meeting on the west side of Chicago. There were sixty or seventy people there. I listened to the speaker and several comments afterward. When we walked out, nothing seemed different, but apparently something was different because I never took another drink and I began to experience the miracle and the power of AA.

In the spring of 1948, I heard Paul S. talk at that same meeting. He was one of the early Akron AAs. Over and over, he kept saying, "AA, in and of itself, is sufficient." I didn't know whether to believe him or not. But, today I believe it's true. AA, in and of itself, is sufficient if we work the Steps.

If I were drowning, I would want a life preserver, not a serving of cotton candy philosophy, theology, or positive thinking. In the Twelve Steps, AA gave me a life preserver. The people in AA told me: "Do these things and your life will change." That is precisely what happened.

Between 1951 and 1958, I worked construction jobs in Thule, Greenland; Keflavik, Iceland; and Point Barrow, Alaska. During most of that time, my AA came out of the Big Book. When the "Twelve and Twelve" was published in 1953, I started reading that. Every day, I read a chapter of the Big Book or the "Twelve and Twelve," and I went through them, over and over. When the Big Book was written, no AA member was sober more than a few years, and yet, its prescription for a sober, useful life remains as timely and powerful today as ever.

After returning to the Chicago area in 1959, I became involved with working in the Cook County Jail in Chicago and the State Penitentiary in Joliet, Illinois. For years afterward, I'd run into somebody at a meeting who had met me, years before, at one of those meetings. At that time, we worked with wet drunks more frequently than we do now.

My first visit to Bill's home was in the spring of 1951, when I was nearing the end of a highly unsuccessful career as a professional wrestler. Television was still pretty new and our shows were just about the only ones on TV that were rehearsed. Sometimes I wrestled at the Rainbo Arena in Chicago. The matches were televised around the midwest and the east coast. It turned out that Bill's wife, Lois, was an avid wrestling fan and used to watch the matches from Rainbo. Immediately, she asked the question all wrestlers dread: "Are the matches fixed?" Well, of course they are, but I kept trying to avoid telling her the truth without actually lying. Finally, I admitted they were, and her face crumpled as disillusionment set in. Another time, at Bill's home, I met Henk Krauweel, a nonalcoholic Dutch social worker who helped start AA in Holland. He said he used to take motion pictures of boozers when they were drunk, and he'd have them watch it after they sobered up. "I would say to them, 'See, you are behaving like little swines,' but they still wouldn't stop," he told me. But when AA started, they stopped.

In 1951, I heard Bill speak at the Medinah Temple in Chicago. He said, "Suppose each of us had not found AA until ten years after we did," and then he paused. There wasn't a sound in the packed auditorium as each of us remembered the despair that filled our souls at the time AA answered our cry and saved our lives.

Bill resisted all attempts by AAs to turn him into a guru or a spiritual lead-

---

FROM "DOES THE TAIL WAG THE DOG?"
June 1999

For me, AA, for more than fifty years, has been like a happy, healthy dog wagging its tail. The tail wag reminds me of a soft sell program existing through members sharing experience, strength, and hope. "What I used to be like, what happened, and what I'm like now" was always the solid basis for individual sharing.

This is what Bill W. saw in pre-Big Book days of AA's infancy. From 100 individual stories, he had heard individual triumphs—one day at a time—over the disease of alcoholism. From these assorted experiences came the foundation for what Bill saw as Twelve Suggestions that others might want to follow. But, they were not to be cast in concrete as dogma because the secret to AA success was that spiritual sharing—without dogma. Here was displayed the basic difference between a fellowship and a religion, emphasizing the underlying reason why, historically, dogmatic religions held scant hope for alcoholics.

Newcomers in AA were encouraged to simply listen to these shared stories and put together their own strengths and hopes. The result, usually successful, was like a happy and sober AA dog wagging his own tail. This was inspired by the simplicity of those individual human spirits sharing their own stories with each other. Each spirit might help another.

Al B.

Gold Canyon, Arizona

er and refused honors from outside organizations. Bill looked and acted like everybody else and in 1955, at the St. Louis Convention, he turned AA over to the members.

I was fortunate to be a guest in Bill W.'s home three times and to be in small groups with him on two other occasions. In retrospect, I'm increasingly amazed at his wisdom and spiritual insight. We don't appreciate him enough. Bill was sober only a few years when he wrote the Twelve Steps. These came to be the foundation of my life as I, very slowly, began to understand their wisdom. The

Twelve Traditions are pure genius in steering AA away from the pitfalls that have impaired so many other spiritual movements.

Alcoholics Anonymous is for alcoholics; it is not for nonalcoholic drug addicts, food addicts, shopping addicts, sex addicts, or any other kind of nonalcoholic. That is critically important and Bill saw that many, many years ago. In fact, Bill explained why a nonalcoholic drug addict does not belong in closed AA meetings in a February 1958 article in Grapevine titled "Problems Other than Alcohol."

That question has surfaced again and again as the treatment industry has sent nonalcoholics to closed AA meetings. Anybody is welcome in AA—provided he or she is an alcoholic. That's very simple, but very important for the survival of our Fellowship. If an alcoholic who also used drugs wants to go to AA meetings, that's fine, but, as Bill pointed out, he should keep his comments to his alcoholism. All addictions are not the same. As a culture, we often worship change and think it's progress. But frequently, it isn't progress, it's simply different.

When Dr. Vincent Dole retired as Class A (nonalcoholic) trustee some years ago, he said, "My greatest concern for the future of AA is that the principle of personal service might be eroded by money and professionalism." The AA message is a message from one amateur to another. By profession, Dr. Bob was a physician, but he helped alcoholics as an amateur. By profession, Bill W. was a stockbroker who helped alcoholics as an amateur. I regularly attend working Step meetings on Wednesday evening and Saturday morning. In the working Step group, the members are committed to working and reworking the Steps. The worst advice I ever got in AA was to work the first nine Steps once and then attempt to exist on Steps Ten, Eleven and Twelve.

In 1963, sober sixteen years, I heard a suggestion that there's great benefit in redoing all of the Steps. It turned out to be absolutely correct. In my experience, AAs who continue to work all of the Steps do not suffer from depression, anxiety, apathy, boredom, and similar symptoms. Today, we have special interest meetings: womens' meetings, mens' meetings, gay and lesbian meetings, and even meetings for doctors, lawyers, and so forth. I've always felt that everybody should be welcome in any AA meeting, even though there may be some use for special interest meetings. I would not belong to an AA group that barred anyone.

My belief in God began as a very simple view of the Higher Power. Gradually, as I read everything I could find on the spiritual life, it became very complicated and, in my view, quite advanced. As years have passed, my belief has become simpler and simpler. My relationship with God is dependent on rigorous honesty and continuing work with the Twelve Steps because this gives me a continuing experience of God in my life.

The Twelve Steps are deceptively simple but provide limitless spiritual growth for anyone with the patience to stay the course. However, the timetable is generally far slower than we believe it should be. That's why so many members of Alcoholics Anonymous wander into various kinds of groups that promise spiritual enlightenment or psychological fixes on a fast track. It's a promise such groups rarely, if ever, keep.

I'm eighty-four years old today, and in all these years, AA has never deserted me, in spite of my frequent wanderings from the program. The AA message is a "spiritual awakening as the result of these Steps." The foreword to *Twelve Steps and Twelve Traditions* says "AA's Twelve Steps are a group of principles, spiritual in their nature, which, if practiced as a way of life, can expel the obsession to drink and enable the sufferer to become happily and usefully whole."

It works for me.

Paul M.
Riverside, Illinois

The Fishing Guide, the Bartender, and Me
September 1996

IT WAS THE second week of May 1945. I lived in Vallejo, California, and I was hung over and sick when I ran into an acquaintance, also a drunk, who asked me how I was. I told her I'd been on a drunk and she informed me that she didn't drink anymore. My ears perked up. "How did you stop?" I asked. She told me that she had joined AA. Thinking that she was talking about the automobile association, I said, "But I don't even drive." "I mean Alcoholics Anonymous," she said. "How does it work?" I asked. "There's a meeting on Monday night; if you want I'll take you." Right away my guard went up. "No, just give me the address and I'll get there myself."

I was married at the time and in the doghouse because of my drinking. When I got home, in order to break the ice, I told my husband (who didn't drink) about this conversation and showed him the address. He offered to take me there immediately—it must have seemed like the answer to his prayers. We were leaving the next day for Jackson Hole, Wyoming, to run a nightclub for the summer season, and on this particular Monday night, friends were giving us a farewell dinner party. The party was much more inviting to me than AA. So I prevailed and we went to the party. During the party he suggested that I excuse myself, tell my friends that I had somewhere to go, and he would take me to the AA meeting. Reluctantly, I went.

The meeting was in a room in the basement of a womens' residence. Everything stopped when I walked in and the three people there welcomed me with much warmth and friendliness. I sat down and the speaker continued with his talk. He talked about living on skid row in Kansas City, begging for money to buy wine. Now it wasn't that I was a high-bottom drunk, but I'd never seen times like that, and I was appalled that this dear, sweet, clean man had to live in such poverty. So that impressed me. The meeting ended with the Lord's Prayer and this really stopped me. I hadn't said the Lord's Prayer since I was a child, and it embarrassed me, so I bowed my head with them but I didn't say anything. My newfound friends said, "You're going to Jackson Hole tomorrow and there isn't an AA group there. May we suggest that you buy this book?" It was *Alcoholics Anonymous*. Thinking that these people were booksellers, but so nice, I bought their book. It cost $2.50.

I took the book and went home to my apartment. It was a time in my life when I could see (I was thirty-two years old then and I'm eighty-three today), and I started reading the book and couldn't put it down. I read until four o'clock in the morning. While reading, it was like a curtain lifted. This was my answer, this is what I had been looking for. Why hadn't I heard about it before? The next day I carried my book along with my suitcase to the car and we drove to Jackson Hole. Stopping at night, I would read the book. A few days later after we arrived at Jackson Hole I noticed that the book gave the name of a woman to contact at the Alcoholic Foundation in New York; her name was Bobbi B. I wrote and told her I was going to be a lone member for the next four months. She answered my letter immediately.

Very shortly after that, another letter came from a sign painter in Salt Lake City, Utah. He was another lone member who had also gotten the book. He wrote that he was going to take a quick job in Jackson Hole just to come and visit me. He came, visited for a few days, encouraged me, did everything he could to help me, and as he was leaving, he suggested, "Why don't you find another drunk and start a group?"

It so happened that in the nightclub we ran, there was a drunken fishing guide. I gathered my courage and I approached him. To my surprise, he was perfectly willing to come to a meeting with me and the next night I decided to have the meeting at the cabin we lived in. I was about two or so weeks sober. I don't know what we talked about. I read him some paragraphs from the Big Book. I didn't even have an extra copy for him, so I loaned him mine (you can see what firm ground I was on). When our little meeting ended, I told him that the group in Vallejo ended with the Lord's Prayer, but that I couldn't say the Lord's Prayer. I asked if he could and he said he couldn't either. I had a portable record player and a record by a famous opera star who sang the Lord's Prayer with much meaning and feeling, so we used it to end our meeting.

When I was about two months sober, my husband was threatening to fire the bartender, who was drunk all the time. I talked with him and he became the third member of our group. We were three drunks who weren't drinking and looking for a way to get well—the fishing guide, the bartender, and myself. We had our meetings during that summer, always ending with the record. (I didn't actually say the Lord's Prayer until I came back, moved to San Francisco, and joined AA in San Francisco.) You have to remember, we hardly knew what we were doing, we didn't have any guidance ourselves, only the Big Book and a power greater than ourselves. We played it by ear. The fishing guide stayed sober and we corresponded for many years. The bartender stayed sober the rest of that season, but I understand when he went back to his home he had some trouble again with booze. I lost track of him after that.

I left Wyoming in September 1945. Getting to San Francisco was a wonderful experience because I made many friends there. I spent about seven years talking to different AA groups that were starting up in the Bay Area. A lot of Twelfth Step work was going on, both one-on-one and also through the central office. The central office would contact the groups to arrange for someone to meet the person who'd called in and perhaps take them to a meeting. Sometimes people would simply walk into a meeting, as I had, and someone would reach out to them, take them under their wing, and offer to become their sponsor. When I saw a need, and I was available to help, I helped.

We didn't introduce ourselves as alcoholics except to new members, and we didn't use our last names. I always simply said I was Vi. It was assumed that if a person wasn't having trouble with booze that they wouldn't be there. Even when someone introduced me to speak they simply said, "I'd like to introduce Vi." All meetings were closed; there weren't any open meetings.

We began our meetings with a moment of silence and the Serenity Prayer. The Preamble was not used then and I don't remember when we started using it. We'd sometimes have a guest speaker. There were no Step or Big Book meetings; all of that evolved over time. It was simple, not structured.

There were just five or six groups in 1945 in San Francisco: the Downtown Group, the North Beach Group, one central meeting on Wednesday night in the Fillmore District, and some others.

The Fellowship was experiencing growing pains, some petty jealousies about one-upmanship, but nothing that wasn't solved easily. I remember how hard-nosed we became when someone came into a meeting drunk. I shudder to think of it today. I remember them escorting a couple of people out. It was like the pot calling the kettle black. Surely if they staggered in they wanted something, they needed something. I was as guilty as anyone; I didn't like the disruption and I caused my share of dissension.

One of the highlights of my life was meeting Bill W. His wife Lois was as charming as I found him. I think I was more impressed with Lois than with him.

In the meantime, my husband, who had so inspired me to go to my first meeting, and I were divorced. AA became my family. I had literally a hundred friends, and it was the greatest experience of my life. In AA I met another man, who is my husband today, forty years later. Both of us have endeavored to live our lives through the Twelve Steps, applying them to our lives.

My husband and I relish the joy of living sober and have many hobbies and interests. We learned how to paint through our local art association, and our home is filled with paintings that we've done. We're not artists; we're simply painters—hobbyists. I had a couple of shows and sold many paintings. Life has been good.

From the time I came into AA in May 1945 until now, I've lived a life of so-briety and happiness. Today I'm almost blind and very deaf, so because of this we're not active any longer in AA, but we still do what we can for people who need AA. We take them, we direct them, we do what we can. My impression, though, of how AA has changed is that we did things more simply when I was young in AA, and to be perfectly truthful, I like the good old days better.

I don't think our founders meant that we had to go to three or four meetings a week in order to stay sober. When I recovered, I reached this plateau in sobriety of security, knowing who I was and where I was going; it was all right to level off. I had no trouble with booze; I became a housewife; I enjoyed my home.

Through all these years I feel I've been blessed: I never had any temptation to drink. A power greater than I am lifted much weight off my shoulders.

Violet D.

Vallejo, California

A Place of Either/Or
April 1999

MY NAME IS Alf and I am an alcoholic. I was born in July 1915, and I had my first drink of alcohol in 1925, at the age of ten. It happened this way. Because of prohibition, moonshine was delivered to customers in tin cans. Our brand was called Minnesota 13, and we supplied Al Capone in Chicago. A young man (who later died of alcoholism) poured a little moonshine into a tin cup, added water, and placed it in my hands. I drank it down and my love affair with alcohol began immediately.

My drinking progressed and during my college days in the 1930s, I first saw tears in my mother's eyes. She and my father came to see me in the county jail where I'd been kept overnight after being stopped by the police while leaving an all-night place called the Bloody Bucket. Perhaps some of you have memories of a place such as that. My road to the pain and darkness that comes with alcoholism had begun.

In 1934, Bill W. was in the hospital in New York, and in Akron, Ohio, Dr. Bob was still getting drunk, even though he was attending Oxford Group meetings. This was also the year when I began attending Oxford Group meetings held at St. Olaf College. Even while getting good grades, I was deep into my alcoholism, knowing that something was wrong and looking for a way to control my behavior while using alcohol.

Attending Oxford Group meetings failed to relieve most of us of the desire to use alcohol, plus most of us didn't care to be preached at about sin and conversion. Pat C., the first AA member in Minnesota, told me how he was living on skid row, heard about an Oxford Group meeting being held at a plush hotel in Minneapolis, rented a cheap suit from a pawn shop, went to the meeting, rejected it all, turned his suit in, got a cheap bottle of wine, and got drunk again. My experience with the Oxford Group was identical with Pat's. I rejected it.

My marriage to Genevieve occurred in 1942, and I was still searching for a way to control the effect drinking alcohol had on my behavior. I read Jack Alexander's article on early AA experience that year, hoping that someday it might reach me. AA had arrived in Minnesota in 1940 when Chan F. from Chicago brought the message to Pat C., and because of him, the good news was brought to me in 1944. Two members with only a few months of sobriety drove a great distance to tell me that if I were an alcoholic, as were they, I was at an either/or place in my life. Either I could continue to drink (and if I were alcoholic, tragedy would enter my life), or I could drive a hundred miles to a home where AA meetings were being held once a week.

The words they spoke were true, but I continued to drink until September 6, 1951, when I surrendered at what I term gut level. There were no AA groups in a two-county area surrounding my home, but an alcoholic with almost a year of continuous sobriety moved to my town, and I called him. The circumstances surrounding this call are called coincidence but to me are a miracle. He told me that all we needed was two persons and God to have an AA meeting. He had no car, so for our first meeting I drove him and his wife to our home. He and I met in our living room and the wives met in the kitchen. At the first meeting we discussed how living the AA way of life would eventually bring balance into the work, play, love, and spiritual aspects of our one-day-at-a-time existence. Our topic came from a small pamphlet printed by the AA group in Akron, Ohio. During the business part of that first meeting, we decided to send five dollars to what we called the "headquarters" in New York City.

It took us a month before we had our third member, but at the end of a year we had about twenty coming to my home. After forty-six years, the group is still in existence. Of those three members, two never drank alcohol again. After many years of continuous sobriety, I relapsed but never stopped going to AA meetings. God was always there for me, and sobriety, one day at a time, returned to me as soon as I became completely honest with myself in all areas of my life.

I served as secretary for the small number of groups we had in southern Minnesota, and in July 1955, the only year the delegates had met outside of New York, I, Genevieve, and our three young children drove to St. Louis for the Second International Convention. There with the delegates seated on the stage, Bill W.

made his talk about all that had happened since 1935 and asked us to vote as to whether or not the General Service Conference should become permanent. The vote was taken, and to me, it seemed a unanimous decision that now guidance and direction of our Fellowship belonged to the members. God as expressed through our group conscience became the ultimate authority for our group purposes, working through the General Service process. I still get a warm feeling when I pass by old Kiehl Auditorium in St. Louis. There I met Bill and Lois W., Ebby T., who brought the message to Bill, Father Dowling, Dr. Tiebout, Sam Shoemaker, Nell Wing, Bill's secretary, and many others to whom we owe a great debt of gratitude. I was elected to serve as delegate for Panel 7 (1957-58), the first elected from that Minnesota area after it became permanent.

So the year 1957 found me at the General Service Conference in New York. My name was drawn out of the hat to serve on the Committee on Conference and Charter. Our small committee held meetings in a hotel room, and Bill was always present. He would stretch out his long legs on the bed and talk about his Wall Street days, his spiritual experience, and his concern that even though AA might change in the future, the Twelve Steps should not. An attorney, nonalcoholic, named Bernard Smith was a great help to our committee. He drew up a document for us which, after being presented on the floor for a vote, was accepted by the delegates. The terms of this document make it almost impossible to change the Twelve Steps.

Another thing we accomplished during my term of service was the removal of the word "honest" from the requirement for membership. Prior to this the requirement for membership had been given as "an honest desire to stop drinking alcohol." Now the doors of AA opened even wider as the only requirement for membership became simply a desire to stop drinking alcohol.

Alcoholics Anonymous was spreading over the entire world. At the Conference I noticed a short bald-headed man sitting not far from me. I asked where he was from. I was told he was not a delegate but an observer for Norway. I'm Norwegian, and he and I became close friends. After the Conference I brought him back to Minnesota to show the few small groups we had that now AA was even in Norway. I hauled him around to speak at many groups in southern Minnesota, and the members were always impressed.

Another example of how we tried to impress early members was how my friend Icky S. from Texas used to do it. Icky was an early delegate and trustee. Part of his drunk story included this escapade. During the war he was a demolition expert, and he continued working with explosives after the war. He received a contract to blow up a bridge. While drunk, he blew up the wrong bridge! Ebby T. stayed at Icky's home for some time while trying to stay sober. Bill always called Ebby "my sponsor," even when Ebby was drinking. In 1966, at the age of seventy, Ebby died sober.

Other memories of the Conference include the delegate who asked our general manager, Hank G., who was conducting the session, "Why do we delegates have to stay in this fleabag of a hotel?" The blood rushed to Hank's face; he remained silent and marched out of the room. In a few minutes he returned and said, "If you wish to see fleabag places, I'll give you a tour within a few blocks of here where I used to stay while drinking." I remember the dedication of staff members such as Hazel R., Ann M., and Nell Wing. In my mind's eye, I can still see us passing our Big Books around for everyone to sign, including Bill. I still see Lois making coffee and Bill playing the fiddle at their home. Other memories: Bill walking around with the manuscript of *AA Comes of Age*, shouting out, "I finally got it finished!"; Naomi B., delegate from Kentucky, and I sitting next to him before his talk about the book, his head bowed and his hands folded as though in prayer. He compared our Fellowship to a cathedral; the Steps being the solid floor, the Traditions becoming the walls holding us together, and a beautiful spire representing our service. Naomi began to cry. Her tears flooding down soaked her dress! Tears of joy.

Years later when I had my relapse, Bill really became my friend through one-on-one visits, telephone calls, and letters. He was never judgmental and assured me that the sobriety I'd had in the past would always be a part of me. During this difficult period, I never stopped going to AA meetings, and Bill always tried to help and encourage me, even getting me certain vitamin tablets at a wholesale pharmacy in New York. They had, he thought, helped his depression. Bill died in 1971, and my last drink of alcohol the second time around did not occur until March 3, 1977, which is now over twenty years ago. I believe Bill knows that I am sober today. When I think about it, I get a glow, much better than the glow alcohol produced at the beginning of my drinking days. Thank you, God.

One last word about my relapse. Bill wrote in the "Twelve and Twelve" that "unless one attains some degree of humility, one is condemned to drink again." For me, humility is being honest with myself in all areas of my life and accepting what I find during the examination of my conscience. I was dishonest in one area, and I drank. Today, in the eternal Now, I am honest in that area of my life, and I have no desire to drink—a gift granted me, I believe, by the God of my under-standing. As long as I remain honest with myself and try to live by the directions given in the Twelve Steps and the book *Alcoholics Anonymous*, I believe the mir-acle will continue.

Alf S.

St. Cloud, Minnesota

—∿∿—

How AA Came to Geneva, Nebraska
July 2001

IT WAS A Saturday evening in April 1964, and usually I would have been up-town at a bar. But I was home suffering from the flu (for a change it was something other than the "brown bottle flu") when a man named Hartley came to visit. My wife reluctantly admitted him to our apartment, believing he'd come to take me out drinking. But Hartley had a different purpose.

He'd seen me at a Lincoln, Nebraska, AA meeting more than a year before, and he wanted to know if I was staying sober. I told him no—"I guess I'll always be a drunk." Then he dumped an armload of Grapevines and AA literature in my lap and asked me to help him start an AA group in Geneva, a rural Nebraska town of 2,300. I couldn't turn him down: it was as if somebody else was doing my thinking for me.

Hartley impressed me with his six-month sobriety token from a Lincoln group but said he had "slipped." Six months without a drink? I believed this man was an authority on alcoholism and Alcoholics Anonymous! I cared not about the "slip." I wanted six months without booze just to see what it would be like.

My visitor gave me some assignments: find a place to meet; write a letter to the New York General Service Office and ask for a group charter and some member-ship cards; write to an AA friend of his who lived in another town for help in spreading the word about the new group; and get a post office box, preferably number 86. I asked why Box 86? Hartley proved his AA smarts to me by saying, "Easy to remember—86 proof whiskey. If you can't get 86, ask for 90."

The local bank was suggested as a possible meeting place, and I didn't mind asking the bank president about letting us use a room. I owed him money on a note I couldn't pay and wanted it extended, and I told him I'd be a better credit risk sober, since we were going to have AA in Geneva. He extended the note, wished us well, but said he had no room in the bank building and suggested I try the courthouse.

So I went to see the sheriff who had put me in jail earlier for driving drunk and then had the nerve to suggest I might be an alcoholic. I told him of our need for a meeting place, but the only spot available was the courtroom. He suggested that the people attending our meetings might feel uncomfortable in such a setting, and I agreed.

Then I made an amends: I told the sheriff I hadn't voted for him in the past because of my jail experience and that I was sorry. Then he told me of his weakness, horse-race betting, and how his wife was constantly on his back. I made friends with this man who also suffered from a wife who just did not understand him!

Next, I was steered to the basement of the library building. To get this meeting room, I had to expose my drinking secret to the librarian—who was the wife of the

---

FROM "THE GIFT IS IN THE GIVING"

April 1989

In the early days of AA in Marin County we were very few and we all tried to handle all the Twelfth Step calls we could get. There were no detox places, no halfway houses, no fidget-farms, no hospital that would take drunks. There was only jail or your own home. We had drunks that peed on the floor, vomited, raised hell all night, then left the next morning to go and get drunk all over again. Some did, however, stay sober and those who did not stay sober at least kept me sober. The ones who did stay sober were the ones who really caused me the trouble. I was run ragged taking them to meetings, keeping them out of jail, getting them back to work, and getting them back together with their families. It took a lot of my time and effort. But it kept me sober and now I have many wonderful friends and memories.

Jim W.
Larkspur, California

editor of the newspaper where I worked. Here I learned my secret wasn't very well-kept, and I got a key to the room, a pat on the back, and permission to smoke at meetings even though the room was also used by the Womens' Club and the Girl Scouts. I had to promise to air it out after our meetings.

The errand to the post office wasn't without incident, either. I used to drink with the husband of the clerk who met me at the window. I told her I wanted to rent Box 86. She said it wasn't available. I asked about Box 90. It also was in use but she did have Box 96 and that had to do. I had difficulty spelling "anonymous" for her. Then she pushed the registration card across the counter, saying, "Jerry, sign this." I said, "Oh, no! This isn't for me! It is for some friends of mine!" She said, "Come on, Jerry, I know you better than that. Sign it!"

Then I remembered the night she had come into the pool hall to get her husband. I begged her to let him stay because he was my partner in a snooker game, but she pinched him by the ear and led him toward the door, with him grabbing for his glass of beer. (At the time, I thought I certainly was lucky to have a nicer wife than she was!)

Things were developing well. In lieu of the charter and membership cards, we got a packet of literature from New York's GSO. The AA member to whom I wrote said that Sunday, April 27, would be fine, and he would spread the word and bring a carload of people with him.

Then Hartley got drunk. He stole a neighbor's check and forged the signature to buy booze, and he was carted off to the state mens' reformatory without a trial because he already was on probation. (Three years later he died of alcohol poisoning in the veterans' hospital.)

April 27 was only a day away, and it appeared I was going to be the lone Geneva drunk on whom the visiting AA members would have to work. So what did I do? I went to a beer joint to find some other drunks.

I crawled up on a bar stool beside a well-liked man everybody called Pappy. This man couldn't handle his booze very well and was habitually being ejected from the bar for throwing up or messing his pants. I bought Pappy a beer and asked him if he had ever heard of AA.

"Oh, yes," he told me. "It is a good outfit. I was sober a whole year down in Kansas before I moved here." Pappy agreed to help me start the new group and concluded the conversation by saying, "Let's go buy a jug, go over to my house, and I'll tell you all about it. My wife is working tonight, and we'll have the place to ourselves."

At midnight, Pappy was having a little nap on the floor. The bottle was empty. I found a pencil and paper and wrote Pappy's wife a note: "Dear Vera, Pappy and I got drunk tonight, but tomorrow things will be different. We are going to have AA in Geneva!" Then I staggered home.

Sunday morning dawned and I was sick. I escaped the house by taking the kids to Sunday school, promising my wife to return to drive her to church, but she knew better than to depend on the ride. She had walked too many times. It took several tomato juice beers at the bar to settle my stomach and nerves. But I did manage to leave the bar in time to get home, clean up a little, and make sure my wife was going to the library with me to make coffee and be at the three o'clock meeting.

Bless Pappy! He was there ahead of me. I was glad to see his smiling face. He told me he had spent the morning finding and pouring out half-full bottles of booze at his place. Pappy was taking this seriously.

The man who spread the word did a good job, and there were thirty-five men and women present, seated around the room in a circle. Someone opened the meeting and the sharing was passed around, each person telling how AA had made life better. Al-Anons shared, too. My wife had only ten cups of coffee in her percolator, and for years these people would agree to visit our group only if we promised there would be enough coffee.

The meeting closed with the Lord's Prayer, but no hat was passed. The AAs told us they weren't taking a chance with our success and didn't want to finance our next drunk. But they did give us three Big Books.

There's got to be a Higher Power watching over drunks. Pappy and I stayed sober from that day on, and within the first year the group grew to five members. Pappy died sober several years ago, and I am the only living member of that original group. AA in Geneva is still alive and well. On April 27, 2000, I visited my old home group along with ten others. It was the occasion of the group's thirty-sixth anniversary and my sobriety date.

Jerry P.
Hastings, Nebraska

A Journey Not A Destination

"We have entered the world of the Spirit. Our next function is to grow in understanding and effectiveness. This is not an overnight matter. It should continue for our lifetime."

"Into Action," Alcoholics Anonymous

No matter how long we've been sober, life continues to happen, and we continue to have only a daily reprieve from our alcoholism. There are no graduation ceremonies in AA. The stories in this section report that sobriety is a journey, not a destination. Over the years, these longtimers tell us, they've continued to learn more about themselves and about how to stay sober no matter what. Sometimes the journey is exhilarating, sometimes rough, sometimes joyous, and sometimes full of trudging. But it is always full of discoveries.

—∞—

The Quest for Spirituality
March 2000

A GOOD NUMBER of years ago, I found myself bewildered and uncertain about the meaning of spirituality and how one achieves it. After a rather frantic search, I fell upon an idea that presented a solution. I realized that by combining Step Twelve, Tradition Twelve, and the last sentence of the book *Twelve Steps and Twelve Traditions*, I had discovered my answer. Let me explain. Step Twelve says: "Having had a spiritual awakening as the result of these steps, we tried to carry this message to alcoholics, and to practice these principles in all our affairs."

To me, Step Twelve says that a thorough digestion of the previous eleven Steps constitutes a concept that could be considered "spiritual." I reviewed each Step and, indeed, found that by embracing all of these Twelve Steps, I obtained a feeling which I call spiritual.

The last part of Step Twelve adds additional clout. It includes two very vital points which make spirituality ring loud and clear within me. By carrying the message to others and practicing the principles of the AA program in all our affairs, Step Twelve rounds itself out for me into a full concept of spirituality.

However, there still seemed to be something missing. Very shortly thereafter I reread Tradition Twelve, which was of enormous help to me in my search for spirituality. Tradition Twelve says: "Anonymity is the spiritual foundation of all our traditions, ever reminding us to place principles before personalities."

It became abundantly clear to me that anonymity was a spiritual foundation not only of Tradition Twelve, but of sobriety itself. When I grasped this concept, it became easy for me to place principles before personalities. As a matter of fact, once anonymity was embraced, the phrase "placing principles before personalities" became unnecessary—it had already happened.

One day, while I was reading the book, *Twelve Steps and Twelve Traditions*, its last sentence jumped out at me and entered my awareness as I read: "We are sure that humility, expressed by anonymity, is the greatest safeguard that Alcoholics Anonymous can ever have."

It followed that humility, as expressed through anonymity, was the greatest safeguard that I could ever have. Thus, anonymity and humility were the core of spirituality—and of Step Twelve and Tradition Twelve. The AA program suggested that we carry this message to other alcoholics and practice these principles in all of our affairs. That latter is a big order, but in the light of anonymity, humility, and spirituality, it became easy to work with others both inside and outside of AA. Now spirituality took on a real, true meaning for me.

Many ask "What is anonymity?" and "What is humility?" To me, they are almost the same thing. They are devoid of prestige; they demand nothing; they don't ask to be "right"; they simply suggest that the icy egocentric elements in all of us retire into the background and that we wear the warm cloak of anonymity and humility and therefore, spirituality.

Earle M.
Walnut Creek, California

—〜〜〜—

Taking Gratitude for Granted
May 2000

FOR A PERIOD of about two years, my daily walks became progressively more difficult. A searing pain in my lower legs eventually became almost unbearable. I found that stopping every block or two and sitting down would make the pain temporarily subside. The best physical therapists diagnosed my problem as stenosis (a gradual closing of my lower spine) and suggested I better get used to it.

A close friend in AA suggested that a doctor at a nearby university medical center might provide some help. I was very doubtful but did go to see the man, who suggested that a surgical procedure on my lower arteries might help. It didn't seem to make sense, but I was cajoled by my friends into the operating theater.

A three-hour procedure which installed stents into my femoral arteries brought about an almost unbelievable change. In two weeks I was walking without pain or strain. I felt remarkable surges of thankfulness as I passed the old "rest stops" without a twinge. I felt real gratitude every day.

About a month later, I found myself home from my walk and in the shower when I suddenly realized I had not noticed any gratitude as I made my round. Nothing had happened—I just had taken the pain-free condition for granted while I thought about other things.

As a result of this experience, it doesn't seem strange to me that I sometimes forget to feel gratitude for my sobriety. After all, it's been forty years since I drank, and it has become easy to take a sober life for granted.

This is why I must continue to work with others, to go to meetings, to be of some service to the world about me—not because these are "good" things, but rather so that I can once again be stimulated into the feelings of gratitude for this life I have found. (And which, for an alcoholic, is so easy to take for granted.)

Clancy I.

Los Angeles, California

—⧈—

The Bottom of the Glass
March 2009

ONE MORNING SHORTLY before my 21st anniversary in AA, I sat eating my breakfast, pleased that I did not have a headache, even though I had eaten some sweets the night before (sugar usually gives me a slight hangover). I reasoned that I felt well because I had eaten some protein with the sugary items. It then occurred to me that, if I ate some solid protein, I could probably have a couple of beers and not feel hungover. Furthermore, I thought, I might not even be an alcoholic; my problems with alcohol could be purely the result of a sugar imbalance. My mind then snapped back to its normal state.

I was appalled and shocked that my brain had produced such a crazy idea. I'd had little "blackouts" before, moments when I would "forget" I was an alcoholic and think a beer was just the thing I needed. But the irrational thought process of that morning was new to me. Unlike the poor sap in the Big Book who thought he could stomach some whiskey safely if he only drank it with milk, I had thought myself immune from such insanity. I had taken pride in thinking that my mental processes weren't as twisted as others'. This was a moment when more was being revealed to me about the cunning—not to mention patient—nature of my alcoholic mind.

When I first considered the concept of "more will be revealed," I thought of the "more" in terms of the Promises—being relieved of fear of people and financial insecurity, knowing serenity, feeling useful and happy. The Promises have

─∿∿─

FROM "THE PAIN HAS MADE ME STRONGER"
October 1998

I do try to rid myself of self-centeredness and to do something for someone each day. Sometimes it's a little thing like letting someone into traffic, or shooting a prayer for the trash men carrying heavy cans on their backs. Once a week I pick up an eighty-eight-year-old lady and take her to the Senior Center to dance. We play opera tapes in the car and hit the high notes, our voices cracking, and laugh our heads off.

Sometimes I slip a few bucks to someone when I know there is a need. If you tell, it doesn't count. Well, now I've told so that cancels that.

Tomorrow is a brand-new day. I'll start out again.

I sponsor two wonderful women and we are very close. They trust me with their fragile feelings and I would do anything for them. What a gift!

I'll be sober twenty-five years in September 1998. Financially I'm not in the greatest shape, but I leave that to God, who has never let me down. I have no fear of financial insecurity. One time I was driving myself crazy trying to find out what God's will was for me so I was running around asking people. One day a person said, "God's will for you is simple. He wants you to be sober; the rest will follow." It did.

Anonymous
Virginia

come true for me, but I've also received much more. In sobriety, I've completed my education, advanced professionally and enjoyed a happy, long-term marriage with another member of our Fellowship. Through working the Steps, I've developed spiritually, made peace with my past and repaired relations with my family. I continue to attend AA meetings because anything I know about recovery seems to have a shelf-life of 72 hours.

In recent years, my understanding of "more will be revealed" has expanded to include some difficult lessons about my limitations and the need for my continued vigilance against the next drink. I first became aware of this dimension of "more will be revealed" when I was 15 years sober. I was going to meetings faithfully, working with others in the program and living a life that was reasonably happy, joyous and free.

But then an internal crisis developed that left me with the same three choices I'd had the first day of my sobriety: drink, kill myself or work the program. Thanks to a loving sponsor, my husband, several close women friends in and out of AA, and the Steps, I walked through this dark night of the soul sober. I emerged with a deeper understanding of my fundamental defects of character and what the daily reprieve promised by the Big Book really means. More was revealed to me about the precious gift of sobriety, the stealthy and lethal nature of my defects and the need for me to work my program as if my life depended upon it.

In the next few years, several long-sober members of my local AA community relapsed. People with a few months or years of sobriety expressed astonishment about such relapses; they could not understand how someone with 16 or 17 or 22 years of sobriety could drink again. They had appeared to have it all together! I would raise my hand at meetings and report that I understood why someone with long-term sobriety might drink again. I was so bewildered and confused, and so afraid of what I knew I was capable of, that I could not guarantee that I wouldn't drink any time soon. I don't know the exact reasons someone relapses. Nor can I fully explain why I might drink again. But I do know that my recovery now feels more precious—and fragile—than it did when I was a few years sober and much less informed about myself.

A long-timer named Gary would say to people who were celebrating double-digit anniversaries, "That's a long time between drinks!" At first I was offended by his words; I thought they were rude and needlessly punctured someone's pleasure in their anniversary. I came to appreciate his comment, though, when I realized it spoke a truth that many AAs can understand. If we stay sober longer than a few years, we will go through one or more dark nights of the soul. These difficult times bring us to new degrees of acceptance and humility because we learn on a deeper level how close we really are to our next drink. If we hang on, we learn how the grace of the Fellowship and the principles of the program carry us through the tough spots as well as the times of joy. Whether we are sober 33 days or 33 years, we each receive our daily reprieve from active alcoholism by working this program to the best of our ability, one day at a time.

Kathleen M.
Providence, Rhode Island

—◆◆◆—

Weeding Out the Crabgrass
August 1984

LONG AGO and far away, I was a young alcoholic. After booting the AA program around for five years, I sat down to take my first sober inventory. That was thirty years ago, and there was not much help available. Worse yet, much of that was contradictory; I was offered the choice of a confession, a case history, or a half-baked self-analysis. It didn't seem to me the founders of AA could have meant any of those things, and Bill W. himself later expressed some dismay at the shades of meaning the members were putting into "nature of our wrongs," "defects of character," and "shortcomings." He said all those were just synonyms for the problems we found during inventory. Fortunately, I had guessed right on that.

It seemed to me that what was needed was the sort of inventory a merchant takes after a disaster, counting up: "This we can use. Those must go before they pollute everything. Sort the rest after the smoke clears." Some members seemed

---

—◆◆◆—

FROM "LITTLE PEBBLES"
May 1999

During those early years, I was still struggling with my racing mind that was full of emotional insecurity, and it seemed to me that no matter what was happening in my life, it was an insurmountable mountain. Thank God for Old Carl, because he told me quite clearly: "No one ever tripped over a mountain—but they sure could slip and fall on a pebble." There it was, right in front of me. Could this really be me—big, proud, arrogant Tony who thought that every time he had a problem it was a damn big one? After that, I decided, hey, wait a minute—I had better start looking at Tony's "little pebbles" and clear them up one day at a time. I did just that, slowly but surely, and finally one day, my mountain was gone. Over the years tiny pebbles started coming back again, but I swept them away a little at a time.

Tony

to be neglecting the first of those categories, and became so sad about all their liabilities that they went out and increased them. I thought there must be something right about me, or my Higher Power wouldn't have fished me out of the trash can just before the lid came down.

Since then, I've Fifth-Stepped quite a few newcomers, trying to help them sort out their garbage, which always seems to fall into three classes: things we did when we were children and then stopped doing; things we did while we were drunk but are not doing anymore; and things we still do that drag us down.

We can make short work of the first, as ancient history, unless we persist in brooding over them; then, we can put down "wallowing in guilt" as a current defect of character. Dealing with the second came easy to me, since I had been a patient in the "Maryland State Home for the Bewildered," as we used to call it. Having been declared medically insane taught me that I was not morally responsible for my drunken antics, any more than a mad dog is "bad." (That does not serve as a legal defense, and if your past catches up with you in court, call it "making amends.") I try to teach newcomers that they can feel regret without feeling guilt.

The third class is the real meat of this discussion. You will find, unless you are a very unusual AA, that your daily life falls rather short of the standards of honesty and integrity we discuss in the evenings. I ask at the end of each day: "What should I have done better, not to win more money, but to feel more at peace with myself?" Whatever it was, I can put it on the list as a clue to a defect of character. Despite all my experience, I do not find my list getting very long; what I see is the same faults creeping back in like crabgrass.

Another clue to defects is overreactions; they are my most reliable guide to unrealistic attitudes and expectations. Are those really defects of character? Not exactly. But they can be the sources of many very real defects, such as false pride, oversensitivity, and intolerance. Again, these remind me of crabgrass; my Higher Power may have cleaned them out once, but it is my responsibility to keep them from taking over again.

A wonderful source of information about ourselves is our hassles with other people. I always consider the possibility that I may have caused the problem. Like any sober alcoholic, I can be pretty abrasive; any pattern that I keep repeating, I have to recognize as "arrogance" or some other lack of humility. We should look closely at anything that impairs our serenity, not simply as a threat, but in terms of "Am I reacting to this in a childish way?" If the answer is yes, then we have another entry for the inventory. I see as my goal living at peace with my Higher

Power, with other people, and with myself, and to me, any behavior that threatens one or more of those is a symptom of a character defect. What I most dread seeing in newcomers is an obsession with "getting even." Some societies regard that as a virtue; but for an alcoholic, it is a terrible drain on peace of mind.

Perhaps the best way to summarize is to say that any behavior or other habit pattern that endangers my serenity is a danger to my sobriety, and can be considered a defect to be identified, tagged, and mowed frequently. I used to say "dug out"; but as time has passed, I've learned that perfectionism itself is one of those "things."

No doubt some purists will say that I'm confusing the Fourth Step with the Tenth, but I don't see it that way. When I finished my Fourth back in 1952, I thought that was it, and I hung up the shovel. But the gradual findings from the Tenth became the building blocks from which I built a better Fourth in 1957. It has gone that way every five years since, and I'm still learning.

When a newcomer brings me a Fourth that looks like a list of the Seven Deadly Sins, I have to tell him that everyone has those, so it is worthless to him. What we need is a list of the rotten attitudes that led to making the same mistakes over and over and over.

A. B.
San Diego, California

—◦◦◦—

What AA Means to Me
October 1998

ON DECEMBER 1, 1968, I emerged into consciousness after having passed out—again. I lay on my couch hearing music and imagining that the flecks in the wooden floor were bugs jumping. I could not be still. My husband told me he really couldn't go on this way. That evening I shamefacedly appeared at the local delicatessen asking for two beers. The knowing look of pity I received as I paid for them was standard among my suppliers. I drank the beers that night truly for medicinal reasons. The DTs were so bad I was falling apart. I called AA. The office was closed but a recording told me when it would be open.

I called the next day, the first day of my sobriety, and they suggested that I come down to the office. That began my journey of continuous sobriety.

Many changes have occurred since then. I have lived in four different states and have come to believe that we develop our own concept not only of a Higher Power but of AA itself. It is true we have a Preamble based on the Traditions that define the Fellowship, but depending on our experience, strength, and hope, we each at any given time have our conception of what AA means.

Today, this is what AA means to me: one alcoholic talking to another without regard for gender, social standing, religious beliefs, age, history, and especially length of sobriety; meetings which follow the AA Traditions of not being associated with any outside enterprise; the ever-evolving conscious contact with God or a Higher Power that is personal, real, and practical, and requires only that I listen; the directions, as written in the Big Book, on how to find a Higher Power and the clarification and explanation of the Twelve Steps as written in the "Twelve and Twelve"; the willingness to follow my path in life guided by my Higher Power; the knowledge that sobriety was freely given to me and that I should freely give what I have to those who want it.

I was attracted to AA because it excluded no one, and I am grateful for the lessons I've learned over the years: that we stop fighting anyone or anything; that it is the details of what I do that make me who I am; that my perception of life is ever-changing and evolving; that the basic "suggestions" I heard when I entered the Fellowship have been a continuous part of my life; that as long as I stay an active member of AA, more will be revealed. God is doing for me what I could not do for myself.

Ruth L.
Portland, Oregon

―∽∾∽―

You Can Always Tell Another Alcoholic
July 2000

I AM A drunk and my name is Bill D. I left Knickerbocker Hospital's alcoholic ward on May 29, 1953. Thanks to the miracle of AA and the Higher Power,

I have not had to take a drink of alcohol since that day. And that is the date I use for my sobriety date.

However, a recent searching and fearless Fourth Step has revealed to me that abstinence is not synonymous with sobriety, although it is definitely a prerequisite.

My late wife, who had a master's degree in clinical psychology, once told me, "You know, dear, at the end of your first year of continuous sobriety in AA, there was only one perceptible change in you. You smelled different."

After forty-six years in the program, I have improved somewhat in the practice of the Twelve Steps. But I have yet to get through an entire day where my every thought, word, and action were governed by Step Three.

"We claim spiritual progress rather than spiritual perfection." Whenever self-will takes over, which is more often than I would like to admit, my behavior is no longer that of a "sober" person.

We have a twenty-four-hour program. The quality of my sobriety is only as good as it is today. In recent weeks, I have had days that, in my estimation, were anything but "sober." It is always easier to take someone else's inventory than my own. I have seen newcomers to AA setting far better examples of sobriety than many of our old-timers, some of whom have up to thirty years in the Fellowship. There seems to be an implicit understanding among them that we can go for days without practicing any of our Steps of recovery, as long as we do not take a drink.

Newcomers often display dedication to the use of the Steps, especially the first three, as well as an interest in and a willingness to perform service as part of their recovery. Some of the older members, on the other hand, seem to have the attitude, "I've got my own recovery, now you get yours."

I've been fortunate. Four and a half years after I stopped drinking, my Higher Power told me to carry the message of recovery into correctional institutions. I have been doing this on a weekly basis since December 27, 1957. In 1974, I helped start an AA meeting for sex offenders in a maximum-security prison. This work has carried me through extremely rough times, including the year in which my wife was killed by an impaired driver, and the time, eleven years later, when I learned within the space of two months that I was legally blind and that I had prostate cancer.

Those alcoholics in prison helped me keep my sanity, since that was one meeting I could never leave feeling sorry for myself. This year I was privileged to

attend the twenty-fifth anniversary of this group, which is now the longest continually running correctional facility meeting in New Jersey.

When I took my first service job, one of the wisest men I knew, Ed S., gave me
a valuable piece of information. "You know, Bill," he said, "you can always tell
another alcoholic, but you can't tell him much." Somewhere in our literature I
read, "The only thing we have to offer is ourselves as examples." This is especially
true in prison service, where the inmates are continually being told what they can
and can't do by those in authority. They have to see us walk the walk, not just hear
us talk the talk.

Before we can be examples, we have to gain the inmate's trust. This does not
happen overnight. It requires months of consistent attendance at meetings. I
learned that one night when it was snowing and I had to cross two mountains to
get to the prison I now serve in North Carolina. My wife begged me to stay home,
but I told her that God's will would never put me in a place where his grace could
not protect me. When I arrived at the meeting that night, I received a great spiritual reward when one of the inmates turned to another and said, "See, I told you
he'd be here tonight."

At last I felt I had attained some real sobriety—at least for a day.

Anonymous
Franklin, North Carolina

—◦◦◦—

A Seat, a Cup of Coffee, and Lots of Love
August 1998

WHEN I CAME to AA in November 1960, having had my last drink the
day before, I came in total terror. Sometime in the middle of October I'd been
released from doing ten days in jail. It was there that I found out I was a heroin addict. Cold turkey is not the way to find out you're hooked on drugs. For
whatever reason, I sat down with a bottle and some money, and said, "Let's find
out who's boss." I found out a week or so later. It was alcohol, not me. I'd lost
again. This was the final straw. There was nothing left inside of me or outside.
I knew that if I took the next drink I would drink compulsively from conscious-

ness to unconsciousness. I was scared as I'd never been scared in my life.

For the time being I did the only thing I could come up with: go to the movies and stay off the streets for a little longer. Postpone the first drink as long as possible. We speak of miracles. I had a thought: Call AA. After leaving the movie I called AA and

---

"THE FOUR OF US"

August 2000

There were four of us. Four women, treasuring our sobriety and wanting more than abstinence from alcohol. We attended the same meetings, listened to each other share, and liked what we heard. But more, we got to know each other and to see the Twelve Steps working in one another's lives.

So we started getting together, just the four of us, gathering for dinner at one another's homes once a month and following dinner with a heartfelt AA meeting. At first, two of us sponsored the other two. But, even with considerable differences in our years of sobriety, no one wanted to be the group guru. Each felt the need for honest feedback to our daily concerns. The trust gradually grew deeper, until at last we knew there was nothing we could not safely share in our after-dinner group. Now each of us has three loving sponsors.

We have shared successes and failures, joys and sorrows, illness and health. In times of stress, the woman in need could count on the understanding and empathy of the other three, just as, in times of celebration, all four of us shared in the joy.

We have had vacations to share, career opportunities to applaud, and both natal and AA birthdays to celebrate. And that brings me to this very day. Today we met in grateful celebration of a total of 106 years of AA sobriety the four of us have, and we are looking forward to 106 years and one day.

Judi C.
Carlsbad, California

said two things I'd never before said: one, I need help, and two, I'm an alcoholic. I was taken to my first meeting the next night. Ten days later, I realized that the compulsion to drink was gone.

I was living in Phoenix at the time and the only meeting around was over in Mesa. One of the men at that meeting came up to me afterward, shook my hand, and said, "Come back, young fellow. We need you." Boy! Talk about setting the hook. I wanted to come back—for all the wrong reasons. For the suits the men wore, and the money they jingled in their pockets as they talked up front. I was hooked on AA, and told everybody within earshot. I did everything backward.

I was without work, though I had a place to stay. Eventually I did get a job. It took me out of Phoenix for twelve days and back for two days. While I was away I was able to get to one meeting a week, until we went up on the Navajo Reservation. Then there were no meetings. Just me and the Big Book. Understanding very little but loaded with energy, I was an absolute pain in the neck. The men in my home group put up with me. They kept saying, "Keep coming back, kid, you're getting there." I wanted to belong so bad, but I knew if they found out who I really was, they'd ask me to leave. As time went forward, I got a job in Phoenix. Now these guys had to put up with me on a regular basis.

At my first birthday in AA, over thirty folks were there to share in my birthday. So many of the Ole Gaffers that I'd come to look up to were there. As I sat down with my coffee, I knew then that I had what it takes to stay. As I looked around the room, I began the slow acceptance that I did belong there and I was cared for, without having to do anything to be accepted. What a relief.

Some two years into AA, I finally met a man and called him my sponsor. I followed Wally everywhere. I was like a puppy. Wally would say something to me and I'd wag on both ends and pee on the floor. Wally began the slow task of getting me to do something about the Steps.

--- ∿∿ ---

An old-timer spoke about the danger of becoming complacent and explained the need for the Steps in her life. "The way I see it," she said, "I might have gotten the monkey off my back, but the circus is still in town." S.E.A., New York, New York

September 2005

Wally died in my third year of sobriety. We both were working out of town at the time. I went to the Arid Club, as that was where we always met on Friday upon getting back in town. Everyone else there knew Wally had died the day before. A couple of men took me on a so-called Twelfth Step call. We went way out into the desert. They stopped the car, got out, and poured me a cup of coffee. One of the men said, "There's no easy way to tell you, Tony. Wally died yesterday." They told me I could run into the mountains and probably never be found. I could run about a mile to the nearest liquor store. Or I could drink the coffee, get mad, be hurt, or whatever. They said that they hoped I'd drink the coffee. I did. You see, there used to be a liquor store about seventy-five yards from the Arid Club. What they were trying to do was give me some time. I'd never been loved or cared about like that in my life. Losing Wally was tough but their care made it a little easier.

Eventually the Third Step appeared on the horizon. Les took me to his home and for fifty hours we talked about God. I finally came to a place where I had my understanding of a power greater than myself, a Higher Power I understood. Finally I had something to put faith in, and it wasn't me. As each of the rest of the Steps were fulfilled, there was a deep sense of consciousness—the beginnings of that conscious contact with a Higher Power. The Steps became the foundation of something so unusual, I still do not know how it works.

From a starting point of terror of the first drink to over thirty-six years of sobriety, a real nice journey. It has not been all peaches and cream. I went to jail in my ninth year. Really stupid. It lasted two days and it was enough. Now I write checks only if I have money in my account.

I am over seven years into my fifth marriage. Four of them were sober. Max is not an alcoholic. I fathered three children and for some fourteen years I was a single parent. That will stretch your patience to beyond thin or breaking. As of today, Max and I have nine children and nine grandchildren. Our children's ages are from forty-four to twenty-nine. Our grandchildren are from fourteen to almost one. Our family is more of a clan than a blood family. Folks become part of our clan because they want to, not necessarily because of blood ties. I've been in business for myself since 1983 and have three college degrees.

In 1974 I was involved in a major motorcycle accident, which left me handicapped, having experienced over 100 fractures to my legs, feet, and hands. While they don't work as well as when I started, I still have all my limbs. The doctors wanted to remove my left foot and right hand in the beginning.

My first sponsor asked that I never waste his time. To this day I have not wasted one moment of the time so freely given me. I haven't always done everything graciously, but I have done the tasks laid out for me by the Steps. What I really miss are those Ole Gaffers at whose feet I sat and listened and absorbed so much. They are all gone, those who played such a major role in the shaping of me in the early years. I have outlived all but my present sponsor, who is very near and dear to me.

I attended the 1965 Convention in Toronto, Canada, but was too new in sobriety to be aware of all that was around me. But the 1995 Convention in San Diego was something else. My sponsor and I attended meetings together; I also attended meetings with those who call me sponsor. I saw that spark of light which we look for. I have it, my sponsor has it, and the others had it. I talked with people from everywhere; I listened to people from everywhere. I was part of everything around me.

To those of you who walk in front of me in time, thank you for your time and patience. To those of you who walk behind me in time, I'm glad you've joined us in this newfound life. To those who have not yet arrived or have left for a time: we will keep a seat, a cup of coffee, and lots of love waiting for you.

Tony L.-B.
San Diego, California

—◦◦◦—

Gratitude
September 1979

THE OTHER NIGHT at our AA meeting, Frank asked a question, and a dozen hands went up. He said, "How do you manage to feel grateful when you're feeling terrible? I can't do it."

George, who has had a stroke, said, "I'm paralyzed in one arm. Soon after I came into AA, I broke the other arm. All I could move was my pinkie. I was grateful that I was sober and that I would recover the use of my broken arm. I'm more grateful for this program every day, for the love and friendship I find here, for my spiritual progress, such as it is—just for being alive!"

Tom said, "I use what I call gratitude-generators. Right at the moment, I have no job, and my wife is divorcing me. But I can generate gratitude by counting my blessings. I'm sober. I'm not crazy anymore. I have a place to live. I'm job-hunting, and I'm praying for the right job. I was sick and crazy and unemployable. I had a mountain of debts. Every morning, I thank God for my good and ask him to let me live this day according to his plan."

I raised my hand and said that I was like Frank. When I have felt depressed, I haven't been able to list my blessings and raise my spirits. "This bit about 'I cried because I had no shoes till I saw a man with no feet' has never worked for me. It's taken time, psychiatry, and a low-blood-sugar diet to get me over my bad depressions."

Then somebody said, "Don't wait till you're depressed to practice gratitude." And that's just it. Gratitude has to be practiced.

I was surprised that I had not thought of this before. I had assumed that some people just found it easy to be grateful. Where had I been all this time? Of course, I had thanked people in and out of AA who helped me over the years. I had been vaguely thankful that I was sober, alive, happy, and free. But now, I realized that I had not been appreciative enough.

The next day, I embarked on my own gratitude-generator. I wrote a list of all the people in my entire life who've taught me something valuable or helped me in some way. I wrote a short description of my relationship with each of them and a brief character sketch. At the time of this writing, I have ninety handwritten pages, and I'm not through yet. Despite years of timidity and confusion, followed by ten years of horrible drinking and antisocial behavior, I have been blessed by so many friends that I can hardly believe it.

FROM "JUST DON'T DRINK BETWEEN EACH BREATH"
September 2000

One of the things I learned from the other members of AA was: "Breathe in, breathe out, don't drink between breaths, go to AA meetings, and the spirit of the Fellowship will guide and keep you forever."

So, in other words, I was told to take it easy. It worked for me then and it's still working for me, thirty-three years later.

Bill G.
Tujunga, California

There was that time when I was seven years old and a cousin of my grandmother's took me for a walk in the woods. She made me stand still and observe what was going on: insects dancing in a shaft of sunlight, birds singing, leaves moving in the breeze. She gave me the gift of special awareness. I wonder whether I thanked her in any way.

Then there was the very rich and famous lady who was at a dinner party on Long Island one night when I got too drunk to drive my car. She took me home with her. The next morning, I woke up in an enormous room overlooking Long Island Sound. Breakfast was brought to me on a tray. Later, I was driven home, having written my hostess a hasty, shaky note. I wish I'd gone to see her years later after I joined AA and while she was still alive. I wish I'd told her what her kindness meant to me, especially since she never said a word about it to anyone.

As I go on writing this list, I remember more and more people to whom I am indebted. And I realize I'll never remember them all. During thirty-four years of sobriety, I've heard a thousand wonderful things that have helped me to stay sober. I wish I could thank everybody—the people who've made great talks, the people who've said something meaningful in closed meetings. Of those I do remember, many are no longer on earth.

My two sponsors, Marty and Chase, are still here, thank God. They are both good friends of mine, and I see a lot of them. I am so lucky to have such sponsors, both gifted with inexhaustible patience and wisdom. Marty nursed me through the worst hangover I ever had, coming off my last drunk. It was in the early days, when medical help for hangovers was not so well developed. Marty said later, "I never saw anybody so sick." She left her office to come to my aid. She sat by my bedside, holding a glass of milk and making me lick the spoon, a process that took about an hour and finally made the turmoil in my stomach subside. Over the years, she has given me well-seasoned advice from time to time, but never unless I asked for it.

Chase has held my chin above the flood countless times when I've been badly depressed. He's said to me, "You have your feet in the clouds and your head in the dismal swamp. Get up and do something. Don't think about it—just do it."

It's easier to express my gratitude to these two, since I'm associating with them. I try to do things for them from time to time. Chase has an eighty-second birthday coming up. I'm going to think up something that will please him.

Writing out this list is a revelatory experience in more ways than one. Sometimes, I've lacked the discernment to be grateful, and I see this now. It's like the story about the man who is floating on the ocean on a life raft. He's praying and praying to God, "Save me! Save me!" Suddenly, he says, "Never mind, God. Here comes the Coast Guard."

Often in the past, my prayers for help have been answered in ways that I have not recognized as answers. Indeed, I have cursed my fate instead of thanking God. I have prayed and prayed, sometimes in desperation, but I haven't thanked him as much as I've implored him.

FROM "MARRIAGE, DRUNK AND SOBER"

February 2003

The path to recovery was not always smooth. Though neither of us took a drink since that night we first read the AA literature, we struggled through periods of depression and fear. We learned that we each had to build a personal program of recovery. We selected different home groups and, most of the time, attended different meetings. It was important for us to realize that we sometimes "played" to each other at meetings or held something back, thinking of the impact on the other. We took different paths in service and sponsored different people. The blessings which came to us through sobriety include adopting two wonderful children (one sober in AA), and an ever-growing international group of friends and relatives in AA. Above all, we have found the true meaning of love and marriage.

In the beginning, it was sometimes difficult to have two sets of alcoholic problems and defects to deal with, but the joy of double sobriety outweighed that. We have learned not to take one another's inventory (even when it is so obvious what would help!), and we've also learned "personal recovery depends upon AA unity." That unity begins at home. We've ceased wondering why all these good things have happened to us and have tried instead to accept them all with grateful hearts—and to pass the gift of AA on.

Jan and Fran P.
Spokane, Washington

So now I have a separate list headed "What You Can Do Now." And this one is very rewarding. I have put down the names of those whom I can show my thanks to, and have written suggestions on what to do. For instance, there's a wonderful friend in Washington, D.C., who was one of my mainstays when I was living there in an impossible marriage. I was wriggling on the end of a pin, so to speak, and she got me off the pin. I had not heard from her in years. The other night, I called her up, and we had a wonderful talk.

There are friends who are no longer here. But in some cases, I can write or phone their children or widows. There's an AA friend's granddaughter, who lives out in Iowa. I have never seen her, but we correspond. In my next letter, I will describe what her grandmother meant to me.

Speaking of that relationship: I am a great-grandmother. I have already spent half a lifetime in AA. You might say to me, "Do you think you have time to get in touch with all your benefactors?" Perhaps not. But I will enjoy doing it a day at a time. And in the meantime, I seem to have generated a lot of gratitude.

F. M.

New Canaan, Connecticut

—∾∾—

Old-Timers in the Making
December 1992

WHILE AT A meeting the other day, I realized that of those present I had the longest period of continuous sobriety. However, that recognition of seniority made me somewhat nervous.

After the meeting the question that kept popping into my mind was, "What happened to the old-timers?"

If I didn't know any better, it would seem there might be an "AA wrinkle ranch" where the old-timers went to retire after so many years of sobriety. Of course, I knew that wasn't true because I belong to a group that has at least a dozen members who have more sobriety than I have, a few in the thirty-five year range.

I knew that it was important for me to find some answers to the question of the missing old-timers, so I began to think about what would qualify a member to be called an old-timer.

When I first came into AA, people in their forties and fifties with twenty years or more of sobriety were looked upon as old-timers. Then, I thought about how people get to be old-timers. I knew that a day at a time, without a drink, like the grooves on a record, sober time builds and begins to race by.

I remember the day I went to my first meeting. I was thirty-eight years old and I had a job. On the outside I looked presentable, but I kept a quart of wine for insurance in the trunk of my car. A couple of weeks earlier I'd made a close to successful effort to take my life with an M1 carbine, but Providence intervened I believe, when one of my daughters came upstairs and opened the door, and I couldn't go through with it.

Although I entered the meeting hall dead in spirit, I immediately got hope from the lively group of people I met. Being brand new to the phenomenon of the program, I was tremendously impressed by people being sober for a year, and those people with ten or more years of sobriety were absolute legends—almost godlike to me.

I began my journey to longevity by joining a group. I became a great inquisitor of my sponsor and other old-timers. I read the Big Book, especially Chapter Five. I became active by setting up tables and chairs, cleaning up after the meeting, and I made coffee for a total of over ten years. I sure got to know a lot of people that way. I also took on the offices of secretary, treasurer, program chairman, and delegate to the intergroup. I was a phone volunteer for three years, and, for my lifetime project, I became enmeshed in the great Twelve Step program we have.

Now, how come I found myself at a meeting with people who all had fewer years of sobriety than I? And where did those legendary old-timers go?

I knew some who had retired and a few who stopped going to meetings altogether (I'm grateful I didn't join those ranks). Some just seemed to fade away, though unfortunately I've been to quite a few wakes of old-timers who died sober and, sadly, I've known a few who went out to drink, ending their lives on a tragic note. A number of the old-timers I know are now working in the field of alcoholism. I did volunteer work in that area and it was very rewarding and not a little humbling.

However, there is another aspect of the program that occurred to me while thinking of the visibility of old-timers; and that was the unusually large number of young people in the program, and the abundance of new groups.

As I see it, what has happened to AA is what's happened to our society; the population has increased one heck of a lot in the past twenty years.

Isn't it a beautiful thing to consider, that the lives of so many people, so many families, are getting well and one day, with the help of our Higher Power, these great masses of new spirits will be old-timers just like me? One day at a time.

Bob C.

South Shore, Massachusetts

The Challenge Of Change

"I see 'humility for today' as a safe and secure stand midway
between violent emotional extremes. It is a quiet place
where I can keep enough perspective and enough balance to
take my next small step up the clearly marked road that
points toward eternal values."

As Bill Sees It

One question can usually start a vigorous discussion among
AA members: "Is AA changing?" Old-timers, who have the
most direct experience of changes in the Fellowship, can
provide a unique perspective on the topic of change. Is it necessary?
Inevitable? Is it always for the better or does it bring risks? In this section, longtimers describe how they deal with evolutions in AA while
staying in spiritual balance.

Not suprisingly, there's a diversity of opinion here. However, there is
general agreement on one matter: that AA's "eternal values" offer hope for
the hopeless alcoholic.

—⦿—

Facing the Future Without the Froth
April 1996

WHEN I CAME TO AA, they told me my Higher Power could be AA as a whole. They told me that a lot, because the only thing that bothered me about this amazing outfit of alcoholics I'd found was the way they went on about talking to God and turning it over. I hadn't had any luck talking to God in a long time; I wasn't so sure that God existed. When I tried to pray I had a strong sense that nobody was listening. But my sponsor helped me to see that booze had been a power greater than any power I could muster to get myself out of its clutches. And I could see for myself that there was a power among these people that was even stronger than the continuing pull of the booze. I could turn my will and my life over to it, and had, almost in spite of myself. And it was doing great things—I wasn't drinking.

So I went to meetings and stayed plugged into the power, and they told me sooner or later it would turn into God, and I could talk to him the way so many of them did. Gradually, with the help of the Steps, I learned how to stay away from the booze, and I learned a lot about living without it, enough to "intuitively know what to do in situations that had formerly baffled" me.

It was a little over thirty years ago that I had my last drink. My Higher Power remains the sense I have that AA is a power higher than I am, and part of a greater whole. I still don't know how to talk to it, though sometimes when I say the Lord's Prayer at meetings that does seem like a good way. I do meditate, and that seems to keep me receptive to it.

But when I'm thinking about the strains on AA's Traditions that I see, like anonymity-breaking and the confusion of AA with other twelve-step programs, treatment modalities, and so on, I can get pretty worked up pretty fast. I don't want AA turned into some New Age refuge for dysfunctionals with endless disorders and a piece of jargon for every human condition. It looks to me as if the rest of the world still respects Alcoholics Anonymous, and I'd like to see it stay respectable in case either of my beloved granddaughters, now very small, should ever need it. And there are other peoples' children and grandchildren to think about too, to say nothing of me.

So I get very passionate in defense of AA and its Traditions. So passionate that my voice sometimes gets shrill, and the old impatience begins to take over again.

Some of my AA friends have helped me to look at this, and I can see that the more upset I get about onslaughts on the Traditions, the more my concept of a Higher Power narrows. I see AA as in danger, and that means that God as I understand it is in danger.

One of my AA friends has diagnosed me as spiritually stuck, and she may be right. I don't feel as if my sobriety is in danger at all but it could be, if I don't learn to separate my concern for AA's future from fear for my own "salvation." Salvation is an odd word to use if, like me, you have trouble calling your Higher Power God or even "him." But AA has been my salvation, and the danger of its dilution by well-meaning souls who want to use AA to heal all the ills of the world scares me, a lot. And you

---

FROM "KNOW THYSELF"
October 1993

After thirty-five years without a drink I find myself very confused about what I'm hearing at meetings.

When I came into AA, I was told I had an illness and if I didn't drink I wouldn't get drunk. Now what I hear is: "If you don't get to ninety meetings in ninety days, you'll get drunk."

"If you don't get down on your knees to pray, you'll get drunk."

"If you isolate, you'll get drunk."

"If you're co-dependent, you'll get drunk."

Recently, I attended a Big Book study group and the group was told by a militant young lady that those who hadn't studied the Big Book with a member of that group would not be asked to join the discussion.

It has always been my belief that no matter how long people are sober, there are no experts. Further, ours is a Fellowship of suggestions and not demands. In my thirty-five years, I have found answers for me but have not acquired the ability to live another person's life.

Marge R.

West Dennis, Massachusetts

can imagine how I react to the notion that anonymity is an out-of-date idea.

A little fear, as lots of us know, can be a good thing. It can motivate me to look at the Traditions and reflect on their importance. But if in the process I get so righteous about anonymity or singleness of purpose that I'm close to frothing at the mouth, I'm doing neither me nor the AA cause any good.

Okay, AA has been my salvation. But I begin to see that it can't be my sole Higher Power. You learn something new every day in this outfit. What I'm working on now is learning more about God, as I try to understand it.

Marcia T.
Tucson, Arizona

—*∿∿*—

Freedom From Alcohol
February 1992

SOMEWHAT OVER THIRTY-four years ago, I came to the Fellowship of Alcoholics Anonymous. I was sick, hurting, angry, and afraid. I remember so well the first meetings, and how I had to sit on my hands trying to control the shaking—how these people came to me, put their hands on my shoulder, and said, "Don't worry, it's going to be all right." Then they took me aside and said, "We know something you don't know because we have been through it, but if you will do the things we say and accept our help, you will never find it necessary to take another drink." Then they sat me down and talked about themselves and got me to tell a little bit about me. As we sat and talked back and forth, I soon found that I was the same as them, had been through the same things, been in the same places, hurt myself and others the same way. I thought, My God, I'm never going to need another drink, and to this date that has proven to be true.

I am grateful that my sponsor was a person who was very well versed in the content of the Big Book and a man who firmly believed in the duties of a sponsor. What this man passed on to me was an understanding of the requirements of sobriety, not the cork in the bottle type we hear so much about, but the real sobriety that comes from practicing the program as it appears in the Big Book—the program that formed the basis of sobriety for our early members and worked so very well for so many years in the Fellowship.

Today, however, such is not always the case. Many times new members are simply left to float aimlessly around the meetings, without ever really finding out about the true nature of their illness and more importantly, about recovery. They aren't given the opportunity to share in the program as it really is and they aren't given the essential tools for change necessary for permanent sobriety. The problem is further aggravated by the infiltration into meetings of material from programs dealing with non-addictive problems—programs dealing with child abuse, codependency, and other hangups. These programs have absolutely nothing to do with sobriety, and as a matter of fact often go in a direction away from the principles of the Twelve Steps. Is it any wonder many of the newcomers are confused, particularly when these things are being brought in by members with some degree of sobriety who should know better?

So where does the problem lie? The Big Book hasn't changed. The program in the Big Book hasn't changed. What has changed is that the message being transmitted at many meetings doesn't accurately reflect the principles of our primary purpose and the message we are asked to carry in our Twelfth Step, the message of having had a spiritual awakening as the result of working the Steps.

All right then, what is the solution? There isn't any sense running from pillar to post, ranting and raving about how AA is going to hell in a handbasket, because all that happens is the creation of a lot of doubt and unrest. But there are things that can be done.

FROM "TRUTH UNCHANGING"

March 1997

I once read that a principle can be defined as truth unchanging. If it is true today, it will always be true. We can practice the principles of the AA program, and age will matter less and less as we continue to grow older and wiser together.

Marie K.
Laguna Hills, California

As an individual I can't control many of the things that are changing but I can help ensure that if there are changes, they will be positive. For example, in a garden we remove or control undesirable weeds; in my personal sobriety, I remove the things that have been blocking me; and in my home group, by means of group inventory, I do something about the things that cause problems.

At the group level, this might mean: 1) ensuring that the message being presented today is as good as the message that was here when we first needed it; 2) seeing to it that everyone coming through the door is given the chance to hear firsthand exactly what it is all about from persons with quality sobriety; and 3) making it known that a group is not interested in all this outside gobbledygook that has nothing to do with sobriety.

We can't be all things to all people, so let's do the thing we do best and that is carry the message of recovery from alcohol. By being knowledgeable about our singleness of purpose, we can do much to help our group and AA as a whole. We can avoid the pitfalls that caused the demise of several other well-intentioned entities that started off with the aim of helping alcoholics, but failed because they drifted from their primary purpose.

It would be beneficial for everyone to realize that AA can only last as long as it remains "a fellowship of men and women who share their experience, strength, and hope with each other that they may solve their common problem and help others to recover from alcoholism." Perhaps the following from a piece of AA literature would help as well: "Sobriety—freedom from alcohol—through the teaching and practice of the Twelve Steps, is the sole purpose of an AA group."

Pinky H.
London, Ontario

———ᘳᕼᘰ———

Portals of the Program
December 2005

TOO MANY TIMES at meetings I hear members say "AA has changed." Well, sure AA has changed. The world has changed too since I entered the door of Alcoholics Anonymous in 1970.

Things were different then. The groups were smaller, cups and ashtrays were washed, floors swept, cake served after the meeting, and there were less discussion meetings. Members were more cohesive and sponsorship was a must.

It dismays me to hear the words "AA has changed," because as an elder statesman (not a "bleeding deacon") it is up to me and my peers who remember "those days" to keep the flame alive. Now we throw away cups, often pay others to sweep the floors, and have no ashtrays. But the spirit is the same. There are plenty of

---

"FOR 'BELEAGUERED CHAIRMEN'"
April 1983

It is becoming increasingly difficult to find a discussion meeting where controversy over dual or cross addiction doesn't crop up. It seems to me that to devote time during an AA meeting to discussing drugs is counterproductive. Dr. Bob and Bill W. used drugs during their drinking days, but discussed only alcohol during AA's formative years. Why can't we keep it simple today?

I once heard a woman at a closed meeting politely told to refrain from discussing drugs. Her reply was: "Please don't turn your backs on me. This program is all I have." This program is all the member who asked her to stick to alcoholism has, too. The latter, my sponsor, has been sober almost thirty years. He doesn't want to turn his back on anyone. We merely want to try to keep AA the most successful program for the treatment of alcoholism known to the world.

AA is nonexclusive. People with all sorts of problems, but who are primarily alcoholics, are entitled to share its blessings. Yet Bill W. wrote in "Problems Other Than Alcohol": "... we have to confine our A.A. groups to a single purpose. If we don't stick to these principles, we shall almost surely collapse. And if we collapse, we cannot help anyone." Those guidelines should help today's beleaguered chairmen, who are loath to quell extraneous discussion lest they appear to be insensitive ogres. Let's try to keep this thing simple.

B. M.

Louisville, Kentucky

jobs to be done to keep the Fellowship open to all and we are the teachers. Time does change things in the natural order of life, but the basic truths and principles that have sustained us through the years remain.

Our newcomers need direction just as older members did upon entering the portals of our program. Who but the experienced are better equipped to do the teaching? I have remained an active member of Alcoholics Anonymous for thirty-four years, attending no less than three to four meetings a week. I also belong to a group, maintain a relationship with a sponsor, and work with others. It is my responsibility to keep basics alive in the hearts of the newcomers: Fellowship, groups (not just meetings), service, and growth through our literature.

It is a phenomenon that a society will often destroy itself from within. Therefore, how wise of our founder, Bill W., to warn us in the Tenth Tradition: "We conceive the survival and spread of Alcoholics Anonymous to be something of far greater importance than the weight we could collectively throw back of any other cause. Since recovery from alcoholism is life itself to us, it is imperative that we preserve in full strength our means of survival."

After years of attending AA meetings and listening to members all over the country and Europe, I have changed, escalated professionally, become educated, solvent financially, have learned to love, respect, empathize, nurture, pray, trust, and realize many of the 137 Promises written in the Big Book of Alcoholics Anonymous. How could I disbelieve that this is a precious legacy left by our cofounders and those early AAs? How could I, as an elder, allow the program to be compromised in any way?

No. "I am responsible" goes far beyond just helping the next alcoholic. It means preservation of our society as a whole.

Pat R.
Bethlehem, Pennsylvania

FROM "SOBER IN THE SIXTIES"
July 2006

One of the aspects of AA I think we've lost over the years is some level of self-respect. Because we were a subculture of sorts, we were careful to be prompt for meetings, to dress as if we were attending work or church, to be attentive during meetings, to not hold side conversations during someone else's sharing, and to hold each other in high regard. Now that AA is a household word and the Twelve Steps have been adapted to address almost every form of social problem, the trade-off may be the casual attitude, expressed in dress and language.

One of the most positive changes I've noticed in the past forty-one years is a higher level of public awareness. As with all things in life, there is growth and growth brings change. One thing remains constant: Sobriety is a gift, a treasure to be cherished, a state of existence that cannot be maintained without the grace of God or a Higher Power guiding each person one day at a time as we "trudge the Road of Happy Destiny."

AA found me. I found a new life in AA, a life filled with challenge, promise, and hope. There have been many times when I've felt inadequate to meet life's demands, but AA and the Twelve Steps have always helped me find a way. I love Alcoholics Anonymous. My fervent prayer for each and every one of us is that AA will be there, one day at a time, forever.

Fairleigh M.
La Mesa, California

The Same Chance I Had
September 2001

I HAD A bad dream last night. I don't know what it was about, but it was a real sheet-twister. Ordinarily, I've been delivered from nightmares, most of my neuroses, and all of my phobias through application of the Twelve Steps in my life. I have a bad night only when I've overlooked something in my nightly Tenth Step. What was wrong?

I'd been to a regular meeting the night before and had noticed a young woman still clutching her court slip. It was a First Step night, and I had made an old-timer's pitch when they called on me: "what it was like, what happened, what it is like now."

In my talk, I had re-upped my dedication to one-on-one sponsorship and sponsors going through the Big Book and the Twelve Steps with pigeons. Indeed, I was eloquent when I reminded the group that times might change, but alcoholism did not. Neither did pitiful, incomprehensible demoralization, nor the language of the heart. I hoped that everyone would have the same chance I had. AA came when I called thirty-one years ago, I said, and my sponsor herded me through the Steps of the program.

"Get a sponsor and get on board!" I said. "Don't be rejected if your first choice says 'no.' We only turn you down if we're too busy with others to be of the best service to you. Ask someone else whose sobriety you admire." I always say that, trying to blunt the fear of rejection that I know too well myself. It was a good pitch.

At the smoke break, the young woman with the court slip had made up her mind. She came to my table and stammered, "Would you be my sponsor?" I didn't hesitate. I said no.

"I couldn't do you justice, dear girl. Too full up. But I'm really proud you asked me . . ." et cetera. "Your sponsor will come along. Just keep looking." What I didn't say was, "And I know the folks who gave you that slip to be signed told you to get a sponsor."

So here I am this morning, cringing at a character defect that once again has me flirting with the bondage of self. Who am I to judge? Did those old-timers in my first home group judge me? Do I want every new person to have an equal chance? Do I want to sponsor only women exactly like myself—desperate women without court slips?

This morning clarity returned. Times change, alcoholism doesn't. I don't remember the young woman's name. Maybe she'll be at the meeting again next week, court slip in hand. Maybe I'll get a second chance to do the job my Greater Power gave me to do, more than thirty years ago.

Judith N.
Marysville, Washington

—⁓⁓—

... And the Wisdom to Know the Difference
June 1994

MANY AA MEETINGS today end with the Serenity Prayer, considered by some members a more inclusive choice than the traditionally Christian Lord's Prayer. Of late my mind has been particularly preoccupied with the last line of the prayer and what it ought to be telling me about some of my own attitudes.

After twenty-seven years in the program, I often find myself thinking about how it was in 1966 when the woman who answered the intergroup phone the day I called took me, two days later, to my first meeting. There were far more men in the meetings then than women, and most of us who came in were much older than today's newcomers. We had had long years of drinking ourselves down to our bottoms—wherever and whatever they were. And the slow passage into degradation, whether in our homes or apartments or in the bars or on the streets, formed a crucial part of our stories, told by speakers at all meetings to remind ourselves of where we had been as well as to help others identify.

To those of us with that background, the youth of today's newcomers is startling and often disconcerting. A large part of it is that drugs—hard drugs—are now almost always involved, and they do in a year or two what drinking took half a lifetime to accomplish. Another part is that a great number of newcomers today, if not a majority, are in or have been in group therapy (as I have), and the "sharing" from the floor often seems indistinguishable from it. There is less of "this is what happened to me" and more of "how I feel today."

Another part is (I sometimes sourly think) that half the population is in one of the so-called "twelve-step" programs that have proliferated to deal with almost every aspect of human behavior, thus removing all stigma from attending AA and rendering it and its many would-be copies "in." Or, in other words, fashionable. Public personalities, ignoring the Twelfth Tradition, announce in the press and on television that they are now in AA.

A well-known political commentator once said of a topic under discussion, "It's far worse than wrong; it's unfashionable." But being fashionable can, in some circumstances, be a disadvantage.

It is easy for someone of my age and generation to think this is not the way it should be; that the young people should be replicas of those of us who came in a decade or two or three ago and the meetings should be exactly the same as they were then.

Common sense points out that no generation is a carbon copy of the previous one, that a history of twenty to thirty years has taken place and that the differences are the result of that. Young people in the meetings today are in many respects luckier: they have learned more in less time. If they seem to dwell at length on how they are feeling at the moment, it doesn't mean they are less dedicated to stopping drinking one day at a time and practicing the Steps of the program. Nor does less shame, brought about by less stigma, mean less dedication.

Even language is different. The words are the same, but the uses are different. If you told the average young person today to take the cotton out of his ears and stuff it in his mouth, you might get at best a slight stare, at worst a poke in the eye with or without uncivil language. An expression from the "Twelve and Twelve" that has raised hackles among some feminist members is Bill W.'s description of the Sixth Step as "dividing the men from the boys," a common expression at the time it was written.

Of course the irony of this is that if the "Twelve and Twelve" had been written in the middle of the last century instead of some forty odd years ago, no one would expect the language to be the same. It's the small differences that get peoples' backs up!

But to go back to the biggest difference of all: thirty years ago the great, binding glue that held together people of widely different backgrounds and educational and social levels was the desperate need of all not to pick up a drink. The only medicine that had ever worked was meetings. There was hardly anyone in a meeting room who had not personally stared disaster in the face. And in those days there were no employee assistance programs and very few rehabs.

I have learned that today when people newly sober or clean leave the rehabs they may also be told to go to AA meetings. Should they protest that pills or hard drugs were the problem, not drinking, they may still be urged to attend AA. This information comes from various newcomers recently out of rehabs. In many ways it's a tribute to the success of AA. But as I see some young people in meetings today, craning around to see who's there, whispering together and giggling after the meeting has started and the speakers begun speaking, my patience, never very great, snaps. I find myself wishing they were watching the speakers with the same hungry need that marked those of us fresh from drinking, and still sweating and shaking. There are other programs for those addicted to cocaine, crack, and heroin. AA should remain for the alcoholic, if not purely alcoholic, then at least mostly.

Having grumbled on now for several pages I find myself remembering what Bill W. said in the course of his last talk at New York Intergroup's annual Bill W. dinner. It was early in my sobriety and I had the good luck to hear him. His subject was anonymity and he spoke movingly. The danger, he said, of forgetting the importance of anonymity, was not so much to the program itself, as to "our alcoholic egos."

There are also the unforgettable words in the Tenth Step: "It is a spiritual axiom that every time we are disturbed, no matter what the cause, there is something wrong with us."

So, is my ever-alcoholic ego engaged and am I having a temper tantrum because the people now coming in are different from the newcomers of my own generation and are not exactly as I'd like them to be?

It's true most of them are less beaten down, but it's also true they got the message and stopped drinking earlier. Some of them—not all—seem to prefer talking about their recovery rather than what brought them there. Alcoholic ego or no, I'd still rather hear the often belittled "war stories" than how well the speakers have done since. I, personally, love to hear about the drunks, the disasters, the firings, the lost years. They remind me of my own. And they are what I want to remember when I pass the kinds of bars (nearly always grungy ones) that sometimes beckon me alluringly. Nevertheless, in the spirit of Bill W.'s talk about anonymity, I must try to remember that because I have a strong view about something, that does not make it cosmic law.

Still, I will continue to seek out the meetings and speakers where I will hear the kinds of qualifications that have helped me stay sober, one day at a time, for all these years, while at the same time keeping in mind the words from the Serenity Prayer: "and the wisdom to know the difference."

In my own case, this means recognizing the difference between my own biases, the result of my age and my experience, and the essential principles that made me sober and continue to help others maintain sobriety.

Isabelle H.
New York, New York

—

Anything and Everything Except Sobriety
May 1998

BY ITS OWN definition, the primary purpose of Alcoholics Anonymous is "to stay sober and help other alcoholics to achieve sobriety." Are we what we say we are, or are we becoming a bunch of phonies? Have our egos let us believe we are something we are not?

Yes, I know that AA is changing in a changing world. Yes, I know that old-timers like me may be out of touch with what's going on in the world around me. Yes, I realize that the AA program has been incredibly useful and helpful in solving many other problems in living. After all, who could miss the trendy message of those who belong to more twelve-step programs than anyone else in the room? So, does that make me a bleeding deacon, voicing alarm for the good of the cause? Or do my observations originate in a valid fear that my lifeline is being eroded?

Increasingly, I find that "problems other than alcohol" are consuming more and more of the focus of meetings in various areas. In Oregon, potsmoking, drugs, sex problems, and family relationships are the principal topics—and they are usually personal rather than general. Individuals are told to share their problems at meetings. This is then the topic for discussion, often followed by all sorts of advice. In Arizona where I spend the winter, the focus is on testifying for what Jesus has done. The "primary purpose of the group" seems to be bringing sober AA members to Christ. A few "spiritual leaders" use meeting time to compare portions of the AA Big Book to passages in the Holy Bible, calling it "the Big Big Book."

It is sad to see some incredibly spiritual Native Americans pushed away because they don't embrace the predominant religious viewpoint. Having been vocal about pointing out page 34 in *As Bill Sees It*, I found myself shunned as a heretic who doesn't understand the AA program. That page contains the following excerpt from a 1954 letter by Bill W.:

"While AA has restored thousands of poor Christians to their churches, and has made believers out of atheists and agnostics, it has also made good AAs out of those belonging to the Buddhist, Islamic, and Jewish faiths. For example, we question very much whether our Buddhist members in Japan would ever have joined this Society had AA officially stamped itself a strictly Christian movement.

"You can easily convince yourself of this by imagining that AA started among the Buddhists and that they then told you you couldn't join them unless you became a Buddhist, too. If you were a Christian alcoholic under these circumstances, you might well turn your face to the wall and die."

The suggestion to close a meeting with the noncontroversial Serenity Prayer instead of the popular Christian Lord's Prayer brought horror to many in the group. One Native American, sober three years, found he could not stay sober under the pressure.

I have no fear about AA surviving this. I know that there will always be a couple of drunks sitting around someone's kitchen table with a pot of coffee and a Big Book, talking about sobriety—though finding such underground groups may be difficult.

So what is my concern? Well, it seems to me that the long form of the Twelve Traditions sets it out fairly clearly. Without AA unity my personal recovery may be in jeopardy. There is no question in my mind that for me to drink is to die. I definitely want to stay alive and be able to carry my own keys.

At the same time, to stay sober, I'm trying to cease fighting anyone or anything. Conflict destroys my personal happiness. The AA program and the Twelve Traditions provide a framework for living, one that makes room for differences in personalities and personal preferences—without having to go to the barricades to defend who is right. In AA it doesn't matter who is right—only who is left! I want to be able to be around for a while longer.

But how about the newcomers? What happens when they get told that AA is something it's not? It's not a place to solve domestic family issues. It's not a place

—◦◦◦—

After sharing my experience, strength, and hope at an online meeting for the first time, I felt very much a part of the growing online world and proudly declared myself an official "cyber-drunk."

"That's fine," an old-timer responded, "as long as you remember you're not a virtual alcoholic."

Anonymous, New York, New York

August 2001

to get advice on how to keep your lithium dosage in balance. It's not a place to learn how to beat the system on drunk driving charges. And, perhaps more significantly, it's not a place to learn how to find Buddha in your liver or Jesus in your heart.

When an AA group conscience loses its primary purpose of staying sober and helping other alcoholics achieve sobriety, is it still an AA group? Does "majority rule" allow an influx of individuals with "Christian hangovers" to change the primary purpose of AA in their area? I never thought it could or would.

Since 1951, I've watched AA transcend barriers of nationality, race, culture, and religion. The bottle never demanded credentials or conformity—neither has AA. Now I observe changes occurring—trendy popular changes that appear to divert from AA's stated and primary purpose. Frankly, it frightens me.

At my age, I can probably make the rest of the trip without undue difficulty. However, I concern myself with those that follow. I have an eight-year-old granddaughter who, if genetics is a factor in alcoholism, is a sitting target for the disease. What will her chances be? Will she one day go to a gathering calling itself an AA meeting and find anything and everything except sobriety?

It is my hope that when AA members call themselves an AA group, they won't create a second requirement for membership. Then our singleness of purpose and our common welfare can prevail. I feel fairly confident this will happen if members of AA will read what is in the basic text for recovery—the AA Big Book. The answers will come. Especially if they practice that slogan, unpopular to some, but important to all: "Think, Think, Think."

Ken W.
Bandon, Oregon

Who's the Boss?
December 1993

MY HEART GOES out to those long-term AAs who have let some of the newer people coming into the program, fresh from the drying-out-studios, become their bosses. What else can it be when these valuable older members stop showing up, feeling they are being "trashed" by the newer ones instead of being respected?

Somehow, though, many of us have never thought of quitting. In fact, quite a few of us with long-term sobriety have felt that whatever contributions we are capable of making could be more important now than ever. So, we're here to stay. And to make clarity and simplicity and singleness of purpose our objectives.

Oh yes, we know firsthand how difficult it is to listen to some of the current philosophies, especially those that mandate that since all addictions are the same, there should be no closed meetings, that anonymity is now outdated, that AA is "evolving" into a world society of linked twelve-steppers who will march off to glory in the sunset.

Indeed, it is difficult for old-timers not to give in to the soul sickness that these fevered fantasies produce. Yes, we are saddened by AA meetings in which psychobabble and other diversions such as wholesale parent-blaming and generational self-pity take the place of the real AA message.

However, in the past couple of years a number of old-timers have set up brand-new groups whose stated objectives are to adhere to AA's singleness of purpose. Our posture is not to fight anyone or anything, even those who seem to abhor the very idea of old-timers. We merely wish to observe the Steps, Traditions, and Concepts. And to hope that others will follow on their own paths to mature sobriety.

So, with AA undergoing changes and with me approaching my thirty-fifth AA birthday, it seems important—vital perhaps—to determine who really is the boss in my sobriety, in my life.

I've sometimes found that it's easier to figure out who's not my boss than to put my finger on who is. I know it's not my checkbook, although it huffs and puffs a lot and tries to be very controlling. It's not my family, although they take a lot of my time. It's not my doctor, who seems to be fond of putting limits on what I may or may not do. Nor is it my church.

It's not my mailman, my favorite service station, the tax collector, my life insurance agent, my restaurant waiter, or the network newscaster—although each of these can spoil or make my day.

Is AA my boss? No, again! Witness the Twelve suggested Steps and Traditions: they are not the Twelve Commandments.

And so, as to who's the boss, we've already got one—a Higher Power. Others need not apply.

John R.
Santa Barbara, California

———

The young man was sharing at an AA meeting. "This hasn't been a good day for me. I wasn't centered, I wasn't in touch with my feelings, and my inner child felt deprived. I just wasn't comfortable in my own skin."

An old-timer leaned over and whispered to the woman next to him, "I'm hard of hearing. What did he say?"

The woman replied, "He says he's hungry, angry, lonely, and tired."

Anonymous

Interviews

"Don't take yourself too damn seriously."

Over the years, Grapevine has conducted dozens of interviews as a way of letting AA members share about their recovery in an informal format. In the following section, you'll hear five old-timers talk about a variety of things: rules and regulations in AA, the effect of weather in northern Alaska, the idea that "nothing ever falls out of the universe," the importance of speaking up in a meeting so we can learn about ourselves, and the necessity of tearing down what Bill W. called "barriers of arrogance." In each case, these old-timers take AA and their sobriety very seriously, but not themselves—Rule 62 in action.

—⁓⁓—

A Living Big Book
May 2006
Liz B. got sober in New York on July 11, 1952, at the age of thirty-one.

How was the AA message first brought to you?

My husband planted the seed. He told me that I behaved like Jekyll and Hyde, and that I should try this AA program. I cursed him out, and he never mentioned it again. To this day, I'm very grateful that he did not beat me with AA. If he had, my nature would not have let me get near it.

I drank another eight to ten months, going downhill.

I had been in the basement for two days praying to die when I took my last drink. "I cannot live this way," I said to my oldest son, who was twelve years old at the time. "You can't depend on me for anything. I'm going up on the Long Island Rail Road tracks and jump in front of a train. I'm just going to end it."

I knew nothing about the Big Book, but a Higher Power came to me the way it says: "He would and could if he were sought." I had never screamed to God so in my whole life: "Oh God, oh God, please help me." At that moment, the message of my husband came back into my mind. That's how I called AA.

How did your husband hear about AA?

Our doctor had already talked to me about my drinking one day while bandaging a finger I had broken. "Mrs. B., please stop drinking," he said. "You're going to wake up and you're going to be very sorry." I walked out of his office and went straight to a bar, where I took all my situations. He told my husband about AA and asked him to go home and tell me about it. He did.

What was your first meeting like?

When I walked into my very first meeting, the girls looked at me and said, "You don't look like an alcoholic." I knew nothing about alcoholism. I didn't know anything about sobriety. I just knew two things: What are we drinking? And what are we chipping in for? That's all I knew. So I started to run from the room. They used to keep two people at the door, and one of the men at the door hit me on the shoulder and screamed at me, "What's the matter with you? Where are you going?" "Those girls said I don't look like an alcoholic," I said. "I don't know what an alcoholic looks like, but I'm about to lose my mind, my home, my children, and everything because of my drinking."

"Have a seat, Sweetie, you're in the right place," he said. They put two tables in the middle of the room that night, and they sat around and shared their strength, their hope, and their experience with me. That very first night, three carloads came to my house to tell my husband about AA. I remember that clearly.

In those early days, what kind of service did you do?

From that first night on, it was Twelfth Step work for me. Any time I got a call, I didn't care what I was doing, I would stop and call another alcoholic and, two by two, we went to the drunks. We picked them up at home, on their jobs, in the streets, anywhere we were called.

How did you work your program?

Basic AA, for me, meant working the Twelve Steps. Remember now, I had three children who were twelve, ten, and five when I came to AA, and a husband. Still, I made seven meetings a week, and three times on Sunday. I picked a tough sponsor. When I'd cry to Flo, she'd say, "Listen, Liz. AA doesn't need you, but you need AA." I cried again after she said that, and then I'd go back and whine some more. Then she'd tell me, and not in such nice words, "Sit on the pot or get up off it." What I say today to new people is, "You're either going to drink, or you're not going to drink."

Did you do any work with institutions?

My sponsor used to take me to prison meetings on a Sunday. After a few years, the jails start calling me. I'd go to Ossining, Mineola, Nassau jail, and the jails here in the city. Wherever they sent for me, I went. That was training I've had that is so fabulous in my life. I hope I don't cry. It taught me to never say no when anyone calls out to me.

I understand that you knew Bill W.

I spoke for Bill's twenty-eighth anniversary.

Where was that?

It was at the Hotel Commodore. There were 2,700 people that night. Bill gave me a Big Book for speaking for him, and in it he wrote, "Dearest Liz, you are a magnificent demonstration of all that is Alcoholics Anonymous. Affectionately yours, Bill."

Did you stay in contact with him after that?

I got thirty-two speaking engagements as a result of that night. I covered all thirty-two. It took me throughout the United States, through all of Canada, and the Caribbean Islands. And until this day, I haven't had time to stay in contact with any single individual, because I'm constantly moving.

And that included Bill?

That's right. But speaking for Bill W. is a memory that I've been hanging on to since 1962. That is a highlight of my life. The pages are turning yellow in my Big Book, but it's still my book. What he said to me in that book has carried me up until today and made me want to live up to it, too, you know? I want to be the Big Book that you see, not that you read. "Don't come up and quote pages to me," I say, "Show me that you're living it."

Is it true you used to see more wet drunks in meetings?

Very true. AA was just a baby, seventeen years old, and hardly anybody had any real length of sobriety, you know?

Some of the wet drunks caused us to lose our meeting places. They would come in and line up on the walls, looking for that coffee, and a cookie, or whatever we would have. And then we'd lose the place because we couldn't throw them off the premises.

There was another thing we did a lot. If you were retiring, or had to be at a wedding, or anywhere there was drinking, you let another alcoholic know. There were times I stood outside of the place, the building. Sometimes we were allowed in if the person could bring a guest, you know? We were always protective of one another. I loved it. At a meeting last night, I was screaming at them, "Get the enthusiasm back! Please put it back in AA."

Talk a little about the changes you see.

I feel them and see them. I'll give you an example. At last night's meeting, I saw a man standing alone. He looked so bewildered. Two guys came over to speak to me. "Do me a favor," I said. "One of you, go over and talk to that man. Don't let that man stand there alone." We never let anybody sit alone or be alone in a meeting of Alcoholics Anonymous. We used to keep two people at the door to greet you. Once you got in, they did not let you out, because they sat on you. Also, when a speaker got up to speak, nobody moved. There was no up and down, or walking in front of a speaker while he or she was talking. We respected each other. I don't care where you had to go, or what you had to do, you did not leave that meeting room until we said the Lord's Prayer. Then you lined up and thanked the speaker.

With fifty-three years of experience, strength, and hope, what's your message for people coming into AA today?

Come in and s-t-a-y. I don't say, "Keep coming back" because new people don't know what that means, and they're in and out like yo-yos. I have a sponsee who has forty-seven years, and she says it's a shame how they're saying, "I'm five days back, and I'm two days back." We didn't have that.

When I came in, it seemed like fifty percent of us made it. Twenty-five percent dabbled a little. And twenty-five percent couldn't make it, didn't have the mind to make it. I always wanted to be in that fifty percent bracket.

What other differences do you see?

Well, I like the change of saying "sponsee" instead of "pigeon." (Laughs)

What was wrong with "pigeon?"

Pigeons dump on you, you know? I like that change. We were very loving and warm with each other. We went to diners after meetings and talked. We sat in cars and talked. We went to meetings, streetcar loads at a time. We went any distance.

How many meetings do you go to today?

I go to five or six a week. Sometimes two a day. I never get away from my meetings. Never.

I told them last night again. I said, "I've never seen anybody in fifty-three years come back and tell me it's so great out there. Not one. That's why I stay, because I'm no different than you, no different than another alcoholic." A man sat next to me not too long ago and said, "I'm back five days." I said, "From where?" I wasn't used to that term. "Well, I lost my wife, my two children, my home, my two cars, and my job," he said. "My God, how did you do that?" I asked. He said that he'd become complacent. That's it. Too many of them graduate, begin to feel good, and they're not used to feeling good. They get into materialism, and they lose it all.

Recovery is your primary purpose in life?

That's right. Stay sober and try to help. That's my main prayer every day when

I'm going out this door. "Lord, help me say something to help somebody," you know? Just let me leave a little seed with somebody. The people love me. There's some that can't stand me, too, which I don't worry about. I walked into a group one night and a girl said to me, "Are you sharing here?" I said, yes. She says, "Well, I don't like you and I can't stand you." I said, "Well, there's two doors, honey. You walk out of either one of those two doors that you choose. You do not have to stay and hear me. Nobody has to." She backed up and sat down. When I finished speaking, she had her hand up. I asked her, "What do you have to say, honey?" "I heard you differently this time," she said. She must have been drunk the first time she heard me. She had to be sober to hear me.

Is there anything you want to add?

Well, I just want AA to stay alive, and for all of us to love and care for each other. I thank God for AA being the powerful Fellowship it is. It is very powerful.

And a blessing. Well, we just can't thank you enough.

I think it works the other way around.

Happy New Year.

No, I say "you," I don't say "year." Happy new you.

—◆◆◆—

The Real Thing

February 2001

Louis M. got sober in 1956 at one of the first AA groups in New York City, the Twenty-fourth Street Clubhouse.

How has your sobriety changed over the years?

(Laughing) It's hard to say. Most of the changes are subtle. They have to do with my relationship to the world and my relationship to others. For instance, I see myself as just a tiny, tiny thing in a physical sense compared to the universe, which a few years ago I worked very hard to try to understand.

How were you trying to do that?

Well, scientists now have an idea that we have 100 or 200 billion stars in our galaxy, the Milky Way. So I would sit down and write the number one billion and try to understand how much that is. I'd think of different things like the leaves on the trees or the grains of sand on a beach and wonder, How many are there? Then I'd multiply by 100 billion and say, "All right, that's how many stars there are." So I got big numbers—zeros that went a couple of pages long—and I'd try to understand that. But I wasn't really capable. I saw the number, but I wasn't capable of grasping it or feeling it.

I came out realizing that as an individual I am so small I'm almost totally meaningless in the universe; it's almost as if I didn't exist. But not quite. In my own small way I'm precious to myself and to the universe, because the universe will never again be the same because I was here and because you were here, because that tree was here or because that leaf was there. As small as I am, I'm not totally meaningless. I once sat on a windowsill because I thought my life meant nothing.

And there's another thing: I do exist. In his Meditations, Marcus Aurelius said that nothing ever falls out of the universe. When I read that, I literally had to close the book and think about it, because that meant me, too. The idea that nothing falls out of the universe gave me a sense of accepting that I belong here, no matter what I think of myself.

So many things have changed over the years. My understanding of the Steps and of some words have undergone great changes. And so it is with the Traditions and everything else in AA. But my sobriety hasn't changed in the sense of my drinking and not drinking. I don't drink and that has stayed the same.

What do you think has altered your perspective the most—meetings, the Steps, or working with others?

I don't differentiate between meetings and what people call "working with others." I don't know what "working with others" means. If it means talking with people, talking with friends, that's no different from meetings. If you are walking along and bump into somebody on the sidewalk, as I'm sure you have many times, you just say hello and sometimes you are there an hour and a half.

To me, those encounters are like meetings. I mean, that's the language of the heart that Bill W. was talking about. Can I tell a little story in connection with that?

Years ago, I used to spend weekends with my family in the Catskill Mountains. They had a little house and a garden, which I liked to work in. Well, one weekend I came back feeling so good that when I got off the bus at the Port Authority, I decided to call my sister and tell her what a wonderful time I'd had. So I called, but there was no answer. Then I tried calling a friend, and he wasn't home. I just stood there hearing the footsteps of all these people walking to work, thousands of people walking, and I wasn't able to tell anyone. And that hurt because when you feel good in yourself it's not the same as when you're able to tell someone else that you feel good.

By the same token, I learned that when I've been defeated and crushed and I'm sad and fearful, it's not quite the same as it is when I tell someone about it.

An old-timer once told me that he believed that AA was a great leveler: When you're up high, your friends help bring you down a little bit. When you're down low, they help bring you up a little bit. And so I've found it.

A lot of old-timers have stopped going to meetings. Why do you think that is?

Well, I don't know too many old-timers who have stopped going. People go less often for various reasons—and not just old-timers. People get sober and they get married and have children, or they get involved in other things. But there are some people, and Bill talked about it, who come to a few meetings and then stay sober and never come back to AA. There are people like that. But that's not the usual thing, and that's not the way I want to do it.

Why do you keep going to meetings?

Do I think I can stay sober without going to meetings? Yes. For how long? I don't know. I mean, I can't measure it or say I can stay sober for four years without going.

Why do I keep going? Not just to stay sober. I know that being sober also involves being with other people who want to be sober. And I like it. A lot of my friends are here, and I like talking with AA people. There's very little bull, as in ordinary society, where you stand around at a cocktail party or something and people say, "It's nice weather we're having, huh?" or they ask, "What do you do?" And they mean, "What kind of work do you do? What's your standing in the community?"

I don't hear much of that in AA. We might talk about the weather or about a ball game, but that's not the main thing. The first thing that captured me at my very first meeting was the way AA members talked with one another. There was a genuineness, something real there, that I wanted. That's what attracted me to AA really, more than physical sobriety. I saw they were sober and that they were honest with each other.

This is still a tremendous lure to me. There's no substitute for it. You know, the thing that Bill later called "the language of the heart." As sick a boy as I was when I came in, I was able to hear some of that language without even knowing it.

What changes in AA do you see today?

Well, one of the biggest things is that we have so many meetings. Mary, one of my early friends in AA, and I talked for tens of thousands of hours in railroad stations, in subway stations, and on park benches. In those days in New York City, there might have been twelve or fifteen meetings from the Village all the way up to West 100th Street. Today, there are 100 or something like that.

We used to say, "Gee, wouldn't it be wonderful if we had meetings every ten blocks?" Well, now we do. I think that's good, although sometimes we get inbred. People don't move out of their territory. I think it would be a good idea if people went to other meetings once in a while just to hear different people, to hear AA with a different accent.

I also think there are a lot more people who know about the Traditions today than there were when I came in. And I think that's a saving grace because without the Traditions, AA is dead.

In the past five years, meetings have been springing up where a single member of AA appears to be a leader of sorts. Do you think this kind of AA works for some people?

I think it's been longer than five years. Sure it works for some people, and in that sense I'm in favor of it. I don't care what anybody does to try to get sober. They have a right to try to get sober in their way.

What I do object to—and very strongly—(it's a judgmental thing to say, but ...) some guys give me the impression that they're the second coming of Bill W., that they're a messiah, you know—the real messenger.

Even then, some people say that they need someone strict to tell them, "Sit down. Do this. Read that." Fine. Sometimes in an emergency that's good, if that's for them. But don't go telling me that this is the way to do AA. That's the dangerous thing. That there is a way to do AA; it's their way. And that includes me. What I say to a newcomer is not *the* way to do it. It's *a* way, and I have a duty to him or her to say, "Now listen to what someone else has to say on this. Get other views."

Some meetings also have a number of rules about such things as the way to dress and the use of swear words. Do you think these rules violate the Traditions?

Yes, I think any rule violates the Traditions. We have no rules in AA according to the Traditions the way I understand them.

Of course, each group is autonomous. The group can say, "Well, if you're not going to abide by this, we don't want you to speak." They have a right to say that, and I do not necessarily have a right to go there and speak. And if I do speak in a way that they don't like they have a right not to like me. I shouldn't get angry at that or resentful about that. So it's a touchy kind of a thing. But to make it a rule and to throw people out if they don't wear a tie when they speak? Does that violate the spirit of AA? Yes, because in AA we have no rules. We don't have rules here.

Do you have any fear about the direction in which AA is going?

Only to some extent. I fear the kind of thing where lecturers come around and say they know the real program. You see, I haven't really done the Steps right, so I don't count. But they have, and they can tell you the real program. That's the very antithesis of what AA stands for. We don't have one big leader. Even in Bill W.'s day, we didn't. And we don't have one clear program despite what some people say about the Big Book.

You know, there are three little sentences on page 164 of the Big Book that the Big Book thumpers never quote: The first two are, "Our book is meant to be suggestive only. We realize we know only a little." The book's writers don't say they know all the answers for getting and staying sober. They don't even say they know most of the answers. They say they know "only a little." Then in the next sentence they say, "God will constantly disclose more to you and to us," which means that as time goes by in sobriety and by talking with one another, we might learn more about staying sober, about ourselves, and so forth. So all the answers in my opinion are not in the Big Book. Far from it.

Was that a great book and a great beginning?

Yes, it was. But all the answers are not there, just as all the answers are not in an individual. It's a constant staying sober and talking to one another in this language that Bill talked about—the language of the heart.

Bill himself said, in connection with the Traditions, that trial and error always have their day in AA. Any way that a person honestly pursues I think is the AA way. It may not work out, you know. Or it may.

So if a great guru comes along and thousands of people follow him, I don't have to pay attention to it. And if they got rid of the Traditions (which would be very hard to do, but it's happened in other philosophical movements that started off the way AA started), would I be sad? Sure I'd be sad. But that doesn't mean you and I couldn't stay sober. You and I could just meet like we used to and talk.

Would I like to see the program go that way? No, because I have an obligation to the guy who's out there drinking today to try to leave something behind for him, so that when he wants to stop he has a chance to get sober. If we keep the Traditions, these little power seekers aren't going to take over and splinter AA into this group and that group.

In general, what Traditions do you see as being least understood and, therefore, in danger of being violated?

The only one that's visible is breaking anonymity at the public level. A year or so ago, I heard a guy on the radio break his anonymity. He didn't want to at first, but he had his psychologist there, and she said, "Oh, you can tell." And he said "Okay. Yes, I'm a member."

I always feel sorry when I hear that. Maybe it seems sort of terrible on my part to say, but they don't really understand what anonymity means or how important it is. Of course, movie stars and other people who are famous violate their anonymity, and yes, people have come in because of that. But Bill W. explains in some of his writings that this whole business isn't about the fact that the great Louis M. has gotten sober.

But as long as the Traditions are there, there are always going to be a few people who take them to heart and that will be the saving grace of AA.

Is there anything else you'd like to add?

Sure. I can talk for another fourteen hours (laughs). You know, I learned more about AA and about myself from *AA Comes of Age* than all the other books put together, except the meeting list. And in it, Bill says that the reason the Third and Fourth Tradition are important is to prevent AA from becoming a frozen set of dogmatic principles, which is like what some of these people say is the real AA. They have a frozen set of dogmatic principles.

When I heard Bill W. speak at his anniversary dinner in the New York Hilton in 1968, he talked about a Buddhist from Japan who asked if he had to understand God the way it was described in the literature. And in effect Bill said no. It didn't make any difference whether the Higher Power was a he, she, it, a cosmic force, or greater humanity.

He also said that there were tens of thousands of alcoholics out there drinking that night, who weren't at an AA meeting because they thought AA was some sort of a cult. They thought they had to come in and become do-gooders. He called on us and he called on me (because when I get involved with a speaker I think the speaker is talking to me) he called on me not to build what he called barriers of arrogance—barriers of arrogance to keep these people out. We have to tell that person, "No, you don't have to do what we do. You're welcome here anyway." The rituals can become replacements for the real thing and the real thing is us talking, one alcoholic to another, in the language of the heart.

Dateline, Alaska

August 2000

Mary Lou S., a native Alaskan, got sober in Anchorage in 1973.

What was your process of getting sober?

I was forty-seven and had discovered that I was drinking, not because I wanted to get high, but because I needed to maintain. I was drinking just to bring myself to deal with my day. I needed distance from my life. I was overwhelmed with the responsibilities I had, and there were a lot. My relationship with my husband had become very difficult, and, of course, I blamed him for my dissatisfaction. He wasn't happy in the relationship either—well, who would be? In northern climates like this, you're kind of trapped together inside during the winter.

I generally didn't drink in the morning. I was usually too hung over. By the afternoon, I was ready for a drink. By this time, I was drinking anything that came along, but I preferred hard liquor. We were certainly making an effort to do our part to support the liquor industry here in Alaska.

We had a big family, a lot of expenses, and not much money. I not only had to take care of this family, the children, the household, but I also wanted to get my education—while I was working. There's nothing like setting impossible goals for yourself! Of course, there was no way I could have achieved that kind of excellence, so everything suffered. I was not in a very good spot.

I thought I was losing my mind. I was glad to find out I was an alcoholic.

How did you hear about AA?

Well, I knew it was one of those things that people do because they're drunks. But to me, it was okay to be a falling-down drunk, not remember what you did at that party or all of those things you said. However, it was not all right to go to AA, because that was admitting something.

And then a friend of mine was struggling as much as I was. We'd get together once in a while, and we'd cut down a bottle of Scotch in no time. She went out one night in a total blackout and drove her car off the road into some brush. This was in Alaska in the winter. The police found her and called her husband. She was just terrified. And a police officer or a friend said, "This is something you might want to look into—AA." So she did. She became willing to try anything. Eventually she realized that what she had was an illness and that she could get help for it. She was thrilled. And because we had been drinking buddies, she passed this news along to me.

What was your response?

I thought it was nice for her, but I didn't know if it was something that I wanted to get into. I really wasn't sick; I was just miserable.

Suddenly, she disappeared from our drinking group and went off to these meetings. She was finding a great deal of help from it, and so was her family. She was beginning to put back together the pieces of a family that had a lot of difficulties. Well, let me put it this way: not back together again, but she was beginning to be able to establish new relationships with people. For better or for worse, she found it more satisfactory than the run she had when she was drinking.

Then my marriage finally went the way some marriages go, and I was alone. I was finally single and able to make my own decisions and live my own life. One night, I was driving and drinking and got arrested. Suddenly I realized that I could have not only hurt somebody but killed somebody. That was a terrible moment when I realized I'd put lives in jeopardy. I decided that whatever my friend had, I wanted some of it. That's when I started investigating AA. I found the right place for me.

And you got sober in Anchorage?

Yes. Anchorage has a good selection of meetings. AA continues to expand and be vital there.

Were there a fair number of women getting sober then, too?

There were more men than women attending the meetings. But yes, we did have a large group of women. At the time I became involved, there was a vital group of women. We didn't have a segregated meeting, but we had meetings that were predominately for women, and we would discuss things that, for the most part, were things that women talk about and not the things that men talk about. But we never closed the doors to men. If they wanted to come, they were certainly welcome. They were usually pretty bored.

Do you feel meetings have changed significantly since you've been sober?

There are a lot of four-letter words these days. I certainly think people should speak the way they feel, but on the other hand, you're with a group and you do need to have some decorum, even if it is an informal group and you're encouraged to be honest. So I found the language has been offensive sometimes, and there seems to be a lack of civility at times. But that doesn't take away from the amount of good work that comes out of AA. It continues to be a program that amazes me, and it crosses all different ages, ethnic groups, and economic backgrounds. Everybody has the same depth of sadness in them.

Do you find that in AA in Alaska people come and go a lot because the state attracts a transient kind of person?

People come up here for all kinds of reasons. They come up for the jobs, seasonal jobs, and the big-paying jobs that corporations offer. They come, they work, they contribute, they're good people, and they seek their dreams wherever they live. Then we have young people who come up just for the summer and go back to college. And we have people who come here because they want to leave behind whatever else is going on and kind of disappear.

And do these qualities surface in AA meetings?

What I hear in AA is a need to connect with other people. And I understand, because many people are thousands of miles away from their nearest family members, so they are alone. And when you're alone, you put in place a support system. Everybody needs that.

What about AA in Alaska at large? Is it pretty much just in major cities, or has it made its way out into smaller towns and rural communities?

It's active all over the state. Almost every small community has some meetings. They're very needed. And they are one of those things that really belong to the community. Meetings are used, of course, by the justice system and corrections as part of their way of dealing with alcohol-related crimes. We have such an epidemic level of alcoholism that we really need to use all of the resources we have—and AA is the backbone of those resources.

Alaska's isolation and weather must play a part.

The weather is a real challenge, especially farther north where there are such horrific storms and winter means business. Those cold, gray days can be very depressing to ordinary human beings who don't have any problems at all.

Does the weather come up in meetings?

Oh my, yes. There's a lot of complaining about the weather, as one would expect. But that's the place where you can do that—to whimper and whine and get it off your chest. There's a chance to ventilate and then a time to take action. And when you live in this part of the world, you have to take action.

Is the native population very involved in AA?

There is a very high level of alcoholism in the Alaskan Native population. They were introduced to alcohol when the white man started coming up here on various explorations. As Native Americans everywhere, they had no experience with alcohol. And so their systems weren't prepared for its impact at all. A native person might get a fifth of bourbon and a couple of pals and just drink it till it was gone, and they were passed out. That was socializing. Alaskan Native people have been devastated by this.

We do have a strong Alaskan Native group. Not everywhere, but here in Anchorage, certainly, there's a strong representation of the Alaskan Native. It's still predominately a white person's group, but Alaskan Natives are a strong component.

Switching gears, how do you feel your relationship to creativity has changed since you've been sober?

I always have had a strong creative track, which has served me well. Sobriety has allowed me, of course, to live. And I no longer have to spend time and energy on all of those things that were going so wrong for me and life. My energy is now my own. I don't have to spend it on being angry and negative. I don't have to be out there trying to blame everybody else for things that are really my responsibilities. And I can take the time to concentrate on being creative. It's a great relief. There's no longer that terrible rush to judgment.

Is there anything you'd like to add?

It's still one day at a time. Every now and then, somebody kind of clips you in the knees, and you just go down. Fortunately, these times have been few and far between, but every now and then, I find myself thinking, Oh boy, I wish I didn't have to go through this without a drink. Fortunately, I haven't had to have a drink for a long time.

Reflections On 28 Years of Experience at Our General Service Office
September 2002

Susan U. was a long-time staff member at AA's General Service Office—at the time of this interview, she'd been working at GSO for over 28 years.

Every AA group is autonomous, so why does AA need a General Service Organization?

Well, we do need a decision-making body for AA made up of elected representatives to collect a sense, or group conscience, of the membership. And it's extremely important to carry on what our cofounders left for us. I can't see it as being done any other way than through a Conference and through the AA World Services, AA Grapevine, and General Service boards.

What changes have you seen in the way AA is organized?

When I came in 1974, the General Service Conference was a little less formal. Sometimes we just had sharing sessions where we would just be able to speak about what was on our minds in a general way. We'd go out and eat, go to our committee meetings, and write up our reports.

It was an exciting time because we were focused on developing literature that would help carry the message, like the workbooks and kits for public information and for work in correctional facilities and with professional communities. The first film produced by AA for the general public was in 1978. It caused quite a stir, because it was so new to work with a producer and maintain anonymity. Now the Conference seems a little more structured, and some Conference members want to spend time deleting a word or crossing a "T" in the literature.

Also, when I was hired, there were all women on the staff. Now, there is an equal number of males and females.

What do you think GSO's greatest challenge is at this point?

I think GSO's greatest challenge is to continue to remain a correspondence office—to answer questions, whether it's by email or letter, on Traditions and other questions and to provide shared AA experience.

But as I see it, the responsibilities of GSO are still the same as when I came here. Part of that, I feel, is the cherished tradition of maintaining the Twelve Concepts and working in partnership with Grapevine. And for both of our corporations to serve the Fellowship, share ideas, and provide a general oversight of the Conference-approved literature.

What would be the harm in GSO's having more authority?

There will always be strong egos and power-driven people who will try to be authoritative. But it never works in AA. Those people are usually straightened out through the group conscience and through a Higher Power. I mean, it just kind of takes care of itself. I've been to 26 Conferences, and you do see a force in these annual meetings where the group conscience does make the final decisions.

Can you give an example of when that was especially important?

The idea of reading the blue card about what you can read at open and closed meetings and about sticking to the topic of alcohol was debated on the Conference floor for one whole day. One group of Conference members wanted to make the blue card Conference-approved. Another group didn't want any card. They felt each group should be able to decide what they want to read at an AA meeting after the Preamble. So finally the Conference voted on making it a service piece, which groups could use if they wished.

Letting go of AA's legal trademark on the circle and the triangle was a big thing in the beginning. I didn't want to see our circle and triangle go to the public, but I could see that AAWS had spent too long defending the rights for people who were using it to sell what I call drunk junk, T-shirts and all sorts of jewelry. That doesn't mean that it's not a symbol of AA, but the General Service Board had to cease defending it.

Some members feel that the New York office wields too much influence over decisions like how contributions are spent to carry the message.

I have heard things like that, and usually it's because someone might be misinformed. However, I feel the delegates and trusted servants who come to the Grapevine and GSO boards now are well-informed and great leaders, and they report the information they receive about the Conference and the Board's activities with a great deal of accuracy, so that there isn't as much of that New York stuff anymore. Most people know that GSO might have some shared experience, but that it has no opinion. The process is quite democratic in thought and action, and the Concepts really are taken very seriously.

I just read an article calling the Ninth Tradition a tourniquet for the bleeding deacon. It's hard not to get adamant when your experience might be useful to people in the present.

I've often wondered what it might like to be an old-timer in a small town and what that person does to keep the spirit of AA alive and at the same time try not to take over the group. The miracle is the spirit of rotation, so that nobody can ever get control of a group. I hope people who find that certain members are trying to run the group will stick in there and try to make it better. But I can only speak for myself: I know I need AA. It doesn't need me. So I'll probably stay in there.

I've often been impressed by the way you sit through staff meetings and, although you have years of experience, really listen to new staff. What helps you maintain such restraint?

I know it's important that new people in AA get a chance to talk, so sometimes I visualize one of the chairpeople of our board, Milton Maxwell, saying, "AA works the best in small groups, where everybody gets a chance to participate."

If you're a member of a large group you might never have to say anything. But speaking up, you do learn a little something about yourself.

Would you elaborate on why it's important to listen to newcomers?

New members of AA are the lifeblood of the Fellowship. Each individual AA member is so unique and so treasured and needs to be met where he or she is.

I'm working with two women now who keep returning to alcohol. And it's so different from what happened to me 33 years ago. I mean, one is on the streets and has multiple addictions. The other lives in a big house and is loaded on prescription drugs, as well as drinking. So, it's very hard for them to focus on the alcohol only. And it's hard for me to just share my AA experience.

Yes, AA has to stick to its primary purpose, but I don't think anybody comes to AA by mistake—most are alcoholic and need help. To me, AA is a magical place. I feel I need to open my mind, heart, and spirit to the new person in the society we're living in now.

What are some of your fondest memories of GSO?

I'll never forget former general manager Bob P. talking about the growing rigidity in AA, to watch out for that. So I've had these things in my heart to try to watch out for, so that we always remember that you can be in AA and be an agnostic; you can be in AA and be an atheist, and you can be a believer of some god in AA.

What do you find yourself thinking about as you near retirement?

I just feel there's so much more that needs to be done, so much more that professionals still need to know about AA. They may know of AA, but most haven't been to an open meeting to really see how it works. I feel it's my responsibility to try to make AA a community resource as much as possible and motivate the CPC committees to do things like sponsoring medical students or seminary students.

Do you have any concerns for the future of AA?

People often talk about AA being ruined from within. I have a feeling that won't happen because of the Twelve Steps for the individual, the Twelve Traditions for our groups, and the Twelve Concepts for AA World Services. It gives me comfort to know that in order to change one word of any of these spiritual principles, all the groups would have to be polled and agree to it.

I also try to remember that it's really about not taking a drink one day at a time. For me, AA is that.

—◦◦◦—

A Fine Old Tree

June 2006

Stony S., a Cree from Regina, Saskatchewan, got sober in AA on May 1, 1959.

How were you introduced to AA?

Thank God for my ex-wife. She told me to phone this chap named Walter. But in fact, there were two Walters. My ex-wife knew they were in AA. I called the first Walter, but he wasn't home. I looked heavenward and said, "Thank God."

Then I tried the next guy. I'll be a son of a gun if he wasn't home. "I'll come and get you," he said. I walked into the meeting room and looked around very meekly to see what the hell was going on there. That's what I remember about the first meeting I went to. I was soaked.

Do you remember your first drink?

Yes. When I had a drink, I was of legal drinking age. But, during that time, Indians weren't allowed to drink in Canada because of the Indian Act. But when I drank, I thought, My God, it's good to be out here doing this kind of stuff.

Were you living on a reservation?

I had moved into the city in 1949. Like many people who aren't allowed to do something, I did it anyway. Indians like me who were introduced to alcohol found holes in the fence and drank anyway.

Did you drink alcoholically from the beginning?

Yes. And even though the Great Spirit would talk to me now and then about my habit of drinking, I wouldn't listen.

Can you talk about that experience?

I believe, whether we're alcoholic or not, we have contact with the Great Spirit at all times. In my case, when I was hung over and sick, I heard the Great Spirit talking to me: "You shouldn't be doing that, my son, you shouldn't be doing that." Finally, he touched me and said, "My son, you've had enough. You'd better follow me. I will take you by the hand and find you a new way of life." He did that as a result of those two phone calls. That was my beginning in AA.

In those first years, what were your feelings about Alcoholics Anonymous?

Well, first off, I didn't even know what AA was back then. I went that first time and sat on a couch along the wall. I heard someone say, "I'm so-and-so, an alcoholic," and "I'm so-and-so, an alcoholic." By God, that made the bells ring in my ears, you know?

I was very suspicious. I thought, If they're alcoholics, what the heck are they drinking? They'd go to the fridge and get milk for their coffee. That's what they were drinking.

When the meeting was over, I thought, Now they're going home to drink. We passed several bars and I wondered why they were going past them. They're alcoholic. Why don't they go in? Are they chicken or what? But Walter took me home and put me to bed. I didn't sleep well because I couldn't fathom the message that was given to me.

When did you start to get some understanding of what was going on?

After about a month, I started to feel the vibrations of sobriety: waking up, having a good meal in the morning, and going to work sober. I think one of the first challenges in my life was the challenge of sobriety—not having a drink because of what I heard at the meetings. Sobriety started to grow on me inside and outside. I started to enjoy life—not totally—but with the warmth that comes from AA.

What about the other legacies of unity and service. Did you do service in those early days?

Oh, yes. Yes.

What did you do and how did you do it?

The older members got the beginners and kind of railroaded us. (Laughs) I started with the fundamentals of a meeting: cleaning up ashtrays, setting up chairs, and getting appointed to make coffee. I thought, This is pretty good. I'll keep doing it because it's taking away that feeling of wanting to drink alcohol. I found out there was a better way of life.

How did you experience unity in the Fellowship?

As the days went by, leading into years, AA grew on me and created a strong sense of responsibility. Many of us guys and gals started establishing roundups, going around the country, and starting meetings. Unity came into play from that.

It was happening all along, mind you. I enjoyed going from town to village to reserve—wherever we started AA groups.

What other kinds of service were you involved in?

I went out with the people who were looking after the facilities. Somebody would say, "Hey, come out to the meeting with us." So, I went out to the correction centers with the boys and gals that went out there.

Were there a lot of wet drunks in those days?

Not a lot, but we did have them. They're quite sparse now but they're still there. The old devil doesn't go away, does it?

What memory stands out in your recovery?

I would say the highlights of my sobriety were the international conventions. I started going to them in 1970 and I've gone to every one since. They have given me a lot of strength.

You were a fairly young man when you came in. How do you think we can attract young people?

When I sobered up, the drug thing was just starting to happen. I'm not being critical, but today it's quite common to hear a young person say they're dually addicted. When I joined AA, you were just an alcoholic. In the sixties and seventies, we got more drug-addicted types of alcoholics. I know a couple of meetings where the old die-hard alcoholics—the dyed-in-the-wool types—say, "We're here to talk about alcohol, not about drug addiction." I guess it rubs them the wrong way, but I really don't give it any thought. If people are there for help, I give it to them.

Do you think it takes away from our singleness of purpose?

To a degree, my friend, although I don't hold many opinions on those kinds of things. It's happening, you know? Live and let live.

How did you carry the message?

Three or four of us Indian boys would get in a car and away we'd go with a couple of white friends. We'd just get out to the meetings on the reservation.

In later years, I saw a lot of younger people at our meetings and thought it would help if I were at meetings and shared experiences in the life of an old-timer. What it's like to be a seventy-six-year-old sober alcoholic. Like an old tree, you know?

An old tree?

Yep. Leaves fall off, branches go bare, and birds don't land on you anymore. You go by the tree, you tap on it, and it's hollow. (Laughs)

What was early sobriety like for you?

After I got a bit of sanity into my life, I realized, My God! I have to live a life that isn't involved with alcohol. I have to learn to live with my family.

That was a big challenge for me. I drank for five years of that marriage.

Did you have children?

Yes, I had four boys and two girls. I thank God that my young sons didn't see me drunk—they were just youngsters. I never drank at home. But it was a challenge to look after them, which I really didn't do when I was drinking. I tried to make amends for all the damage that was done.

You got divorced?

Yes. In 1970. I remarried in 1974. We have two daughters who have only seen me sober.

You have had some health problems?

I think of them as challenges. The first challenge came from not realizing the damage I had done to my body, to my organs. I didn't know that any damage was being done because of my drinking. I used to get this pain in the side where my liver is. There was a lot going on in my body. Appendicitis. Alcohol affected my liver. As a result, although I had quit drinking, I had an operation and, darn it, I came back to life again, because I just about died.

What kind of work did you do after you got sober?

I did carpentry work or plumbing—if I could find work in construction. After the operation in 1969, I tried to go back to plumbing and pipe-fitting, but my strength was gone. So I went to work in the field of alcohol and drug abuse.

As a counselor?

My shingle said—get this—"Education Consultant."

Well, you knew a little bit about drinking and getting sober, Stoney, so that fits. You did that work for how long?

About fifteen years.

Do you still go to meetings?

I'm handicapped. On January 1, I had a leg amputated.

Do people come by and bring you a meeting?

Yes, they do.

You've lived a full life and have helped many alcoholics.

Well, God willing, I think I did. I hope I did, anyway. I give thanks to the men and women of AA, and most of all, to the Great Spirit.

Making It New

"I have become a pupil of the AA movement rather than
the teacher I once thought I was."

As Bill Sees It

If newcomers are the life blood of the Fellowship, it might be said that old-timers are its heart and soul. But while it's clear that beginners in AA have a special claim on our attention, it is less frequently acknowledged that longtime sober members face their own set of difficulties.

Old-timers are, like everyone else in AA, only one drink away from a drunk, but some AA members may assume they have all the answers. Longtimers may be more reluctant, therefore, to talk about personal upheavals or say "I don't know." A desire to drink, a failure of faith, a period of depression—old-timers may keep these to themselves. In addition, they must avoid complacency, which can lead back to a drink. And, although old-timers can be a repository of wisdom, they sometimes wonder whether their experience is helpful or even heeded. They care deeply that the AA message survives to help new generations, but they don't want to find themselves preaching.

In this section, you'll read some of the ways that old-timers renew their commitment to AA and remain teachable—how they "make it new"—even after many years of sobriety.

Taking the Time to Listen
December 1997

"DECK THE HALLS ..." danced in the air as I walked into the club where our AA meetings are held. I was glad to be there. It was a chance to see many familiar faces, a breather from the "normal" world.

I felt particularly good, with a "I've-just-done-a-good-deed" kind of feeling. Mentally I had done an inventory. I'll share it with you: First, I had over three years of working as a temporary sponsor resource person. I'd worked on the archives committee for the state convention. My one-on-one sponsorship was adequate. I greeted visitors when they attended our meetings. I drove people to meetings, to detox, and to treatment centers, and went on Twelfth Step calls. I collected clothes for AAs at the rescue mission and spoke at rehabs. I'd become immersed in helping the sick, suffering alcoholic. Yes, I felt good.

Did I have a tiny flicker somewhere in my heart that something was missing? If so, I ignored the feeling.

The meeting began and many of the smiles on those faces changed as members shared the pain of the season. It seemed that the very joy pouring forth in carols, well wishes, and colored lights was the catalyst for sadness.

I heard stories that touched my heart. Not pity-pot stories but stories of life: relationships broken, jobs lost, children ill, confusion that replaced the sane thinking of someone with long-term sobriety. Mental illness plagued one, cancer another. Their stories were no less tragic than the alcoholic detoxing in a downtown center.

I saw them as if for the first time. Then God nudged me: "Look around you. These people need love and support. Charity begins at home." I thought of the times I'd given a home group member a quick hug and sailed out the door to help a newcomer. The term, "If it doesn't work at home it doesn't work" took on a new meaning. The members of my home group are my family.

The sick, suffering alcoholic sits in my chair, sits in the chair next to me, or across the room. Newcomers don't have a corner on being sick or on suffering. Maybe my hands don't shake as they once did. I can actually get the coffee cup to my mouth without spilling it. I may look strong but I'm not; my strength depends on my spiritual condition, which depends on my attendance at meetings and for that I need you.

After all these years I still may not say how I really feel. I may fear rejection. My head monsters may be dragging me around by my thoughts. I may still say, "I'm fine" when I'm dying inside. If I hide my pain, the others probably hide theirs, too.

Now when I look into the eyes of the person next to me and ask, "How are you?" I will take the time to listen. I want to keep in mind that at any given time, each of us may need the same love and support as someone who is attending their first meeting.

Sandra E.
Jacksonville Beach, Florida

FROM "GARDEN HOSE SOBRIETY"
October 2006

At church one day, the preacher said, "I am just a cheap, ordinary garden hose. The water that comes from me and waters your spiritual garden is not from me, it is from God. I am merely a conduit."

It dawned on me: AA never needed my "support." All my good works were really nothing, because I wanted to claim the credit. I wanted to be the Big Man on campus. That was a terrible mistake. When I effectively practice my program, I am only a cheap garden hose carrying God's message of hope, recovery, and forgiveness. Neither Bill W. nor Dr. Bob tried hanging on to the notion that they got drunks sober. They believed they were used as agents of a Higher Power to serve his will.

When I go to a meeting today, I no longer have the delusion that I am supporting a good cause. I need AA; AA did quite well without me during my ten years of self-exile. I go to AA meetings today to hear and see how God is working. When I share at a meeting, it is not to try and "help" those poor wretches, it is because I need their help and guidance.

When I don't share at a meeting, I listen intently to let my fellow recovering drunks know that God is listening to them through me, that God is being there for them through me.

Jeff M.
El Paso, Texas

—◦◦◦—

An Old-Timer's Checklist
June 1989

WHEN I WAS sober less than a year in Alcoholics Anonymous, I longed for the "prestige" of five years. As I approached five, I yearned for the "recognition" of ten and fifteen. At twenty-five, and later, there've been moments when I've had no doubt that I had "arrived." Papa Ego was glutting himself on a menu of attitudes until he was fairly bursting at the seams.

I have found myself expecting all kinds of acknowledgment simply because of my sober longevity. It was only recently, when I met a contented man, sober thirty-nine years (I actually became tongue-tied!), that I started to think about my length of sobriety in terms of what Bill W. called "unrealistic expectations." I got out the old, dusty inventory pad and headed up the page "Self-centeredness, aka Unique-ness and Big-shotism." Here are some of the questions I asked myself.

Am I long-winded at meetings, imagining that I "owe it to the group" to talk at length in order to share my exclusive store of experience, strength, and hope?

Do I get annoyed when I am not called on or when I am not listened to? Maybe I don't show it, but do I think it or feel it? My drunkenness was a selfish experience but recovery is a group activity. We all get sober together or none of us get sober. There are a lot of us at meetings and common sense ought to tell me (and it will if I listen) that everyone at a discussion meeting cannot always be called on.

Do I expect of myself that I utter gems when I share and expect that you will take my "wisdom" to heart? I need to remind myself that wisdom is not all that hard to come by in AA. Wisdom begins the first day for each one of us and grows with our sobriety.

Do I expect my home group to keep me in office because of my "vast experi-ence"? When I take a minute to look at the record, I see that it was made possible for me to hold office in my early AA life thanks to the fact that older members ro-tated out. They showed me, by example, that they cared enough about me to give me the same chance they had been given. They also showed me something about humility: They didn't get swelled heads and act as if they were the only ones who could do the job.

Do I try to manipulate group events (as I did in the beginning), using my length of sobriety as a weapon?

In social settings, do I pretend to information and worldly experience that I imagine I should have because I am an AA old-timer?

Does it occur to me that more success on the job—and more money—would be forthcoming if only my employers knew exactly who I was?

Do I get impatient with long lines at the market, bank, or gas station and imagine that I should be allowed to go to the head of the line because, after all ...?

In failed relationships, do I take full blame because I've been sober a long time and should have known better? (Even non-alcoholics know that usually in these situations more than one party is at fault!)

Do I quietly meddle in the lives of my friends, believing that I can solve their problems because I have apparently solved the major problem in my own life?

Thanks to this mini-Fourth Step and to an ongoing Tenth, I am happy to report that Papa Ego has gone on a diet and his weight is stabilizing.

W. H.

New York, New York

Why I Keep Coming Back
May 2001

MOST PEOPLE HAVE a few days in their past that stand out in flaming colors. They are marked by signal events that were either so bad or so good that they became unforgettable.

One such day for me was April 15, 1950. You could call it a very bad day because I had been drinking for the previous week or so and was trying to medicate my awful feeling of sickness with several bottles of beer. You also could call it a very good day because it was the last time I ever picked up a drink. Fifty years have passed, but I still have deep gratitude for the recovery from alcoholism that followed in Alcoholics Anonymous and continues to this day.

I was only twenty-four then, which at the time was considered young for AA, and this made me feel different, even in the Fellowship, where people bend over backward to accommodate anyone and everyone.

Drugs were not part of the scene when I was drinking, but I suspect that I could easily have become a drug addict. In a military hospital in 1949, I was given morphine for three days following surgery. This was such a flight in ecstasy that I almost fought the nurses for more. Had there been a place called Joe's Morphine Saloon outside the hospital gate when I was released, that might have been my first stop. I got drunk instead.

Like most AA members, I take no personal credit for my sobriety. Nor do I feel that I have it made in staying permanently sober. In fact, many of us in AA say that we are "recovering" rather than "recovered," which implies that getting well is an ongoing, day-at-a-time process. If we deserve any personal credit for getting sober, it should probably be for tenacity in staying with the AA program in spite of all the troubles, frustrations, and boredom we might face. While most of us do find a measure of happiness and some peace of mind, we also have to deal with the problems that confront all human beings. There are very few people anywhere who have trouble-free lives full of absolute bliss.

Many of us feel fortunate in having had a problem that forced us to seek help, which has been a great advantage in our lives. If AA members have any advantage over non-alcoholics, it's in having the marvelous Twelve Step program as a guide for living.

It surprises some people that AA members continue to attend meetings after years of recovery. But I find at least three good reasons for this practice: first, it helps me maintain and enhance my personal sobriety; second, I can contribute to, and benefit from, AA's caring community; and finally, I can stay close to the spiritual ideas which are the basis of our Twelve Step program.

If AA members are firm and unyielding on one point, it's our shared conviction that alcoholics have a lifelong problem that can be arrested but never cured. "We are like men who have lost their legs; they never grow new ones," the AA founders said. While this extreme view of alcoholism is occasionally challenged, our experience seems to show that it's true. And AA members who have picked up the bottle after years of abstinence have, to their sorrow, confirmed it.

It's also true that many people discontinue AA meeting attendance without returning to drinking. But I like to play it safe. AA has worked so well for so many years in keeping me away from the bottle that I don't want to change anything. It is very easy to establish a routine of attending from one to three meetings a week—and this keeps AA in the forefront of my life. I also take every opportunity to remind people that a long time away from the bottle is no guarantee of continuing recovery; there is always the danger of lapsing into overconfidence or indifference.

A few months before his death in 1961, the eminent psychoanalyst Dr. Carl

—*◌◌◌*—

FROM "MORE WILL BE REVEALED"

October 1998

[Thirty years later], this is what AA means to me: one alcoholic talking to another without regard for gender, social standing, religious beliefs, age, history, and length of sobriety; meetings which follow the AA Traditions of the ever-evolving conscious contact with God or a Higher Power that is personal, real, and practical, and requires only that I listen; the directions, as written in the Big Book on how to find a Higher Power and the clarification and explanation of the Twelve Steps as written in the "Twelve and Twelve"; the knowledge that sobriety was freely given to me and that I should freely give what I have to those who want it. I was attracted to AA because it excluded no one, and I am grateful for the lessons I've learned over the years: that we stop fighting anyone or anything; that it is the details of what I do that make me who I am; that my perception of life is ever-changing and evolving; that the basic "suggestions" I heard when I entered the Fellowship have been a continuous part of my life; that as long as I stay an active member of AA, more will be revealed.

Ruth L.

Portland, Oregon

Jung said in a letter to Bill W. that alcoholics have an unmet spiritual need that is part of their problem: "I am strongly convinced that the evil principle prevailing in this world leads the unrecognized spiritual need into perdition, if it is not counteracted either by real religious insight or by the protective wall of human community. An ordinary man, not protected by an action from above and isolated in society, cannot resist the power of evil, which is called very aptly the Devil."

"The protective wall of human community" describes AA for me. To outsiders, an AA group may seem like a ragtag bunch of people who smoke too much, overdose on coffee, and still have too many problems to be called well-adjusted or in any sense recovered. But to most of us in the Fellowship, AA is a caring community that is now worldwide. I've attended AA meetings in many parts of the United States and Canada, and it's always the same: people who care about helping one another find and maintain recovery. It is also a community of people who understand how others can be trapped in deep loneliness and despair. Being a part of this caring community is so important to me that I can't imagine getting along in life without it.

AA, along with building a protective wall of human community, also has a spiritual program which is outlined in the Twelve Steps. The spiritual side of AA has been difficult to explain and is sometimes used by alcoholics as a convenient excuse for rejecting AA's help. But many older members—myself included—view the spiritual program as AA's rock-solid foundation. Some of us even go overboard in thinking that these spiritual principles may eventually have a role in saving society and the world, though Bill W. warned against such egotism.

It is satisfying to believe that AA's work with alcoholics is making some improvements in society, however. Every recovery, though it may go unnoticed, improves the world in some way. We say that AA saved our lives, but it may also be saving the lives of people who never touched a drop. Every AA recovery, for example, is one less person who may be driving drunk or causing havoc in other ways.

How effective is AA in helping the majority of alcoholics? We have no magic wand to influence those who are not ready to change their lives. But I am convinced that the recovery rate is very high among people who have a burning desire for a sober way of life and are willing to go to any lengths to accept and practice AA's ideas. The AA pioneers had this same belief, which is repeated at many of our meetings: "Rarely have we seen a person fail who has thoroughly followed our path. Those who do not recover are people who cannot or will not completely give themselves to this simple program, usually men and women who are constitutionally incapable of being honest with themselves. ... There are those, too, who suffer from grave emotional and mental disorders, but many of them do recover if they have the capacity to be honest."

That's what I was on April 15, 1950—a person suffering from grave emotional and mental disorders that had exploded into alcoholism within a few short years. After a seven-week stay in a Nebraska state mental hospital, I went out to face a world that still seemed harsh and chilly. By staying close to AA's caring community and distancing myself from even one drink, I've been able to live in a different sort of world, and one that has become noticeably warmer. After fifty years, AA still works for me, and even the mental and emotional disorders no longer seem so grave. And there are at least two million recovering alcoholics world wide who can say the same about their own lives.

Mel B.
Toledo, Ohio

Online And Active
May 2003

FOR SIXTEEN YEARS, I was an active member of AA, doing all the usual stuff: going to several meetings a week, sponsoring people, enjoying service work in many different capacities, and meeting with AA friends throughout the week. I have always loved meetings (they have never been a "must" for me), and have been blessed with a host of dear friends in the Fellowship, including my husband, whom I met in AA. Together our spiritual and social lives are centered in Alcoholics Anonymous.

Then, a little over four years ago, with no discernible warning, I was struck by several severe illnesses and struck hard. I suddenly entered into what has been, up to now, the most difficult period of my entire life. I became so critically ill that I was barely able to eat or drink, let alone attend AA meetings. I came very close to death. This is not how I had envisioned my early forties, or any time of my life, for that matter. Yet, as always, life must be lived on life's terms. Suddenly, I was unable to do hundreds of things that I had done before. The losses were, and are, beyond description. And do you know what I missed the most of all? Fellowship. My meetings. I felt so sad every time another meeting passed at my home group without me there. I was struggling to survive, and I needed the sustenance of my AA friends and seeing the program at work in their lives. I needed the reminders that "I am not alone," that with HP we can walk through whatever comes our way, and all the other great blessings that fellowship brings into our lives.

At first, my husband and I hoped that this would be a short illness, but that has not been the case. After seven months without a meeting, I was desperate. I got on the phone, and the outcome was that a small group of women began to come to my home once a week. These women brought hope and love to me for two years, and we all benefited from our meeting, until each of our lives changed and that meeting had to come to an end.

Fortunately, in the meantime, I had put aside my "contempt prior to investigation" and obtained access to the internet and joined two online email meetings. This was a scary step for me, because I was afraid of the internet and dubious about online meetings. But I knew it was important for me to try.

Now, I have been blessed by the joy and fellowship of Alcoholics Anonymous once again and in a new way. This May I will have been sober twenty years, the last four of which have been maintained solely by online fellowship (and literature, including Grapevine). Contrary to my fears, I have found very good sobriety online. I have done a more serious and in-depth study of the Big Book than I ever did in face-to-face book studies. I have made several close friends before and after the meetings, and we have cherished and enriching friendships, despite the physical distance between our homes.

Although most of my AA friends have been supportive of me, I have also heard small rumblings of criticism about online AA and how it is harming or threatening to harm our great Fellowship. I beg to differ. Quite honestly, if I could go to my home group tonight, I would be there. I would so love to get the hugs and smiles and tears in person that I can only read about online. But that does not mean that my online meetings are "less than" or "not real AA" or any of the other criticisms that are, I believe, based in fear. I cherish these online meetings just as dearly as the face-to-face meetings I wish I could attend.

I believe that if there are people avoiding face-to-face meetings and "hiding out" online, they are not the kind of people who are active online either. They would not suddenly overcome their shyness, resentment, or fear, and show up at face-to-face meetings if they were forced to by having no online AA to go to. The people I know who are active in my email meetings are people who always have chosen to be active in AA. They are, like me, ill and very grateful to have meetings they can still attend on the internet, or they are people who are active both online and at face-to-face meetings (as I hope to be someday).

In the meantime, I have found plenty of opportunities for service in Alcoholics Anonymous online: there is no shortage of newcomers and not-so-newcomers needing support and love; there are always jobs that need doing. The Twelfth Step is being worked in a myriad of ways among us, along with the other Steps, Traditions, and Concepts of our program.

My Higher Power has once again given me the tools I need to stay sober and to live as comfortably as I can with unresolved difficulties. If possible, my sobriety has grown even deeper and more meaningful to me during the last four years, partly because of my experiences, which have drawn me very close on a daily basis to my HP and taught me a lot about present-moment living, acceptance, compassion, and patience. Definitely, my life has been enhanced by the sharing and fellowship I find here on my computer, twenty-four hours a day, seven days a week.

Please do not be afraid of online Alcoholics Anonymous. As in meetings every-where, there are positive and negative folks, newcomers and old-timers, wisdom to be shared, and friends to be made online. Alcoholics Anonymous is alive and well on the internet; as usual, it's all a matter of perception. Looking through the lens of deep gratitude, I see a new medium that has given me the opportunity to be an active and vital member of this great family of Alcoholics Anonymous, a family who has saved my life and continues to enhance it daily.

Kris M.

Chino, California

A New Way of Looking at Life
April 1981

ONE AFTERNOON A few months ago, I found myself reviewing the story of AA cofounder Bill W.'s encounter with cosmic consciousness in Towns Hospital. I had come across a well-detailed account of the incident and had not proceeded far into it before I began to experience feelings of envy. After all, I reasoned, why shouldn't I have my own "mountaintop" ecstasy? I longed to achieve the awareness Bill described, to discover for myself the essential unity of the created world.

I failed to realize at the time that my own negative attitudes had long prevented me from viewing the world and its activities in a consistently benevolent manner. By now, I am honest enough to admit that, even after the drinking stopped, instead of finding delight in the wholesome aspects of life, I had too often been captivated by the sufferings and drudgeries. Fascinated by the seamy side, I had singled out the appearances of injustice, overreacted to them, and often concluded in desperation, "What a hell of a mess the world is in! God, is it possible that you exist?"

Oh, there was something in it for me, or I wouldn't have done it. But that sort of pursuit is the stuff dry drunks are made of—if, indeed, the recovering alcoholic is fortunate enough to stay off the sauce. But I attended meetings and worked the Steps; improvements set in; and on this particular afternoon, I was blessed with a comfortable outlook on life.

I found myself able to recall vividly the living hell of those last months of drinking and to see the contrast between the pleasant times I had been enjoying recently and the pain of those final encounters with John Barleycorn. After all, I had very nearly died and was now restored to good health, had lost nearly everything and was currently the recipient of all that was really necessary for a full life, had recovered my mental capacities to an amazing degree, and had experienced more sustained peace within than I had found in over thirty years of striving. Feelings of gratitude came easily that day. As I continued to reflect on these matters, an exciting insight occurred to me. It promised to be a real breakthrough, and I was noticeably quickened.

The insight was related to my intense enjoyment of music. You see, the sounds of an orchestra playing a symphony of Mozart, for example, can send me into orbit almost anytime I might hear them. I experience a marvelous high without booze. When I am under this spell, the inner harmonies and beauty of the sounds are readily apparent to me—overwhelmingly so! The reaction comes easily, I suppose, because I've studied music, worked at it, and listened to a lot of it. Yet to someone who is a bit tone-deaf or is uninitiated, the sounds of such an ensemble are perceived as irritating noises or even bedlam. I know this to be true, because people who feel that way have told me so. I have come to understand that my own positive response to music, affording me so much joy, is truly a perception of my own, a product of my inner attitudes and conditioning.

At this point, the meaning of the analogy I was developing became clear. I realized that my life and the lives of those around me do, in fact, form their own parts in a symphony of interaction. To see it right, I would probably have to include the entire universe within my view, but I was aware that my attitudes and the limitations of a finite mind prevent me from perceiving the spiritual design in it all—just as tone-deafness prevents the hearer from appreciating a symphony. The way I am put together, I am led astray by shallow considerations, trivial distractions, irrelevant observations.

Yet that day, I knew God was in his heaven and all was right with the world, because, on looking back over my own life, I could trace the influence of a Higher Power. Too many good and interrelated incidents had happened without even my cooperation. I was able to sort out the significant events of my life quite well with the aid of hindsight.

After a bit more reflection, I was forced to conclude that although my spiritual rebirth in AA had been a gradual awakening rather than a single ecstatic event, I had indeed been granted far more awareness of the action of a Higher Power in the world than I had previously admitted. How wonderful to be sober, to be able to think clearly (at times, at least), and to become aware of some portion of the greater wisdom concealed so deeply within myself.

And isn't that what this program is really about? Acquiring transforming attitudes, gaining a more spiritual perception of life, and maintaining it so that we can live comfortably—even experience some highs without the artificial aid that is such a deadly poison to us. We gain through AA a new way of life—a new way of looking at life.

D. J.

Columbus, Ohio

—◦◦◦—

Reciprocal Strength
January 1998

IT'S ALMOST FORTY-seven years since AA entered my life and changed everything. How was I to know that sobriety would last so long? It appeared at first to be just another weekend on the wagon. My previous experiences in heroic self-restraint had a shelf-life of about a week. Why should this one last any longer?

I'm now eighty-two. I was a cynical, thirty-five-year-old drunk on that Thursday in August 1950 when, although I didn't know it, my life was to be changed. I've likened that transforming instant, when despair gave way to a glimmer of hope, to a tiny flower sprung into bloom amid the bombed-out wreckage of my life. Thanks to AA, that tiny bloom was to become a garden.

Of course weeds have occasionally popped up in my garden, but I haven't had a drink, nor have things ever become as bad as my life was before I met Alcoholics Anonymous.

Well, here I am. My eyes aren't working as well as they used to, but I'm still capable of shaving before I go to meetings. I'm grateful every time someone drives me to a meeting hall, for it is then I feel very grateful, knowing that I owe my life and happiness to the AA program. What more can life give to an old duffer?

As a result of my life experience, I can tell those people who are still noodling on the fringes of AA to get with it and forget their "maybes." The AA life is real. And enjoyable. And it lasts.

I know a diminishing number of members who have forty to fifty years of sobriety and we are the best of friends. But it is the young people—those one-to-fifteen-year members who had still to be born after I attended my first meeting—

where I find my strength in AA. That strength is reciprocal; it flows back and forth between us. I feel it as the warmth of a meeting again sweeps over me.

And I know that while I am in no way special, my life has proved that I have much to give of what, two generations ago, AA people so freely gave to me. Although mine is an old gift, it is still worthwhile.

Jack M.
Vancouver, British Columbia

FROM "THE BEST IS YET TO COME"
July 2006

A long time ago, I read in Grapevine that it's not enough just to go to a meeting, sit, then get up and go home. All through my AA journey, I have been active—washed ashtrays and cups, served as secretary of meetings, and put my hand out to newcomers with a smile. I have visited hospitals and prisons, carrying the message of recovery in AA, and all this action has kept me comfortably sober. At the end of the Promises on page 84, the Big Book states, "They will always materialize if we work for them."

Today, after more than thirty-four years in AA, I still go to six AA meetings a week. I always sit in the front row, nodding my head up and down, identifying.

"You've only just begun," my sponsor said on my fifth birthday. "The best is yet to come!"

"You've only scratched the surface!" he said and smiled when I celebrated ten years.

"You ain't seen nothin' yet!" I heard at twenty years. At thirty years, an old-timer-said, "Now it's going to get better and better!"

I can't wait until my next birthday, when I hit thirty-five. "Better, and better, and better!" someone will probably add.

If it gets much better, I'll bust.

Hal R.
Millbrae, California

*An old-timer was overheard describing the way he works his AA program:
"I go to meetings, read the Big Book, and work the Steps. When I think
I have it all figured out, I throw out everything I think I know and I start over."*

C.
Springfield, Illinois

THE LAST WORD

Words of Wisdom
May 1998

Charlie W. hadn't achieved forty-six years of sobriety without developing a strong sense of the Steps and Traditions, and the intuitive thought described in our Promises.

Jack, the newspaper editor in Charlie's hometown, had proved himself an enthusiastic—if uninformed—friend and admirer of AA. He kept pressing Charlie to share his years of wisdom with readers through an interview—anonymously, of course.

Charlie continued to refuse the interview, contending he couldn't speak for AA, or even for his group. But the editor continued to plead until, one day, Charlie relented.

"Here," Charlie said, "is the wisdom I've gathered from forty-six years of active and sober participation in the program of Alcoholics Anonymous." And he leaned forward with great confidentiality: "Alcoholics Anonymous, Jack, is a fellowship of men and women who share their experience, strength, and hope with each other that they may solve their common problem and help others to recover from alcoholism. . . ."

Jack's pen scribbled furiously on his notepad. "The only requirement for membership is a desire to stop drinking."

The pen flew. "There are no dues or fees for AA membership, Jack; we are self-supporting through our own contributions."

Jack's jaw was going slack with the wisdom of this man. "You see, Jack, Alcoholics Anonymous is not allied with any sect, denomination, politics, organization, or institution. It does not wish to engage in any controversy, neither endorses nor opposes any causes. Our primary purpose, Jack, is to stay sober and help other alcoholics to achieve sobriety."

Wow! Away ran Jack with his interview, and, meticulously guarding the anonymity of the old-timer, he ran the interview in full.

AA members read the story in belly-laughing admiration of the adroitness of the old-timer. The general public got a straight-from-the-book definition of what AA is and is not.

And Charlie W. sat back with a quiet prayer of gratitude that his group recited the AA Preamble from memory at the beginning of every meeting.

Ralph M.
Heavener, Oklahoma

The Twelve Steps of Alcoholics Anonymous

1. We admitted we were powerless over alcohol—that our lives had become unmanageable.

2. Came to believe that a Power greater than ourselves could restore us to sanity.

3. Made a decision to turn our will and our lives over to the care of *God as we understood Him.*

4. Made a searching and fearless moral inventory of ourselves.

5. Admitted to God, to ourselves, and to another human being the exact nature of our wrongs.

6. Were entirely ready to have God remove all these defects of character.

7. Humbly asked Him to remove our shortcomings.

8. Made a list of all persons we had harmed, and became willing to make amends to them all.

9. Made direct amends to such people wherever possible, except when to do so would injure them or others.

10. Continued to take personal inventory and when we were wrong promptly admitted it.

11. Sought through prayer and meditation to improve our conscious contact with God, *as we understood Him,* praying only for knowledge of His will for us and the power to carry that out.

12. Having had a spiritual awakening as the result of these steps, we tried to carry this message to alcoholics, and to practice these principles in all our affairs.

The Twelve Traditions of Alcoholics Anonymous

1. Our common welfare should come first; personal recovery depends upon A.A. unity.

2. For our group purpose there is but one ultimate authority—a loving God as He may express Himself in our group conscience. Our leaders are but trusted servants; they do not govern.

3. The only requirement for A.A. membership is a desire to stop drinking.

4. Each group should be autonomous except in matters affecting other groups or A.A. as a whole.

5. Each group has but one primary purpose—to carry its message to the alcoholic who still suffers.

6. An A.A. group ought never endorse, finance or lend the A.A. name to any related facility or outside enterprise, lest problems of money, property and prestige divert us from our primary purpose.

7. Every A.A. group ought to be fully self-supporting, declining outside contributions.

8. Alcoholics Anonymous should remain forever nonprofessional, but our service centers may employ special workers.

9. A.A., as such, ought never be organized; but we may create service boards or committees directly responsible to those they serve.

10. Alcoholics Anonymous has no opinion on outside issues; hence the A.A. name ought never be drawn into public controversy.

11. Our public relations policy is based on attraction rather than promotion; we need always maintain personal anonymity at the level of press, radio and films.

12. Anonymity is the spiritual foundation of all our traditions, ever reminding us to place principles before personalities.

AA Grapevine

AA Grapevine is AA's international monthly journal, published continuously since its first issue in June 1944. The AA pamphlet on AA Grapevine describes its scope and purpose this way: "As an integral part of Alcoholics Anonymous since 1944, the Grapevine publishes articles that reflect the full diversity of experience and thought found within the A.A. Fellowship, as does La Viña, the bimonthly Spanish-language magazine, first published in 1996. No one viewpoint or philosophy dominates their pages, and in determining content, the editorial staff relies on the principles of the Twelve Traditions."

In addition to magazines, AA Grapevine, Inc. also produces an app, books, eBooks, audiobooks, and other items. It also offers a Grapevine Online subscription, which includes: new stories weekly, AudioGrapevine (the audio version of the magazine), the Grapevine Story Archive and the current issue of Grapevine and La Viña in HTML format. For more information on AA Grapevine, or to subscribe to any of these, please visit the magazine's website at aagrapevine.org or write to:

AA Grapevine, Inc.
475 Riverside Drive
New York, NY 10115

Alcoholics Anonymous

AA's program of recovery is fully set forth in its basic text, *Alcoholics Anonymous* (commonly known as the Big Book), now in its Fourth Edition, as well as in *Twelve Steps and Twelve Traditions, Living Sober,* and other books. Information on AA can also be found on AA's website at aa.org, or by writing to:

Alcoholics Anonymous
Box 459
Grand Central Station
New York, NY 10163

For local resources, check your local telephone directory under "Alcoholics Anonymous." Four pamphlets, "This is A.A.," "Is A.A. For You?," "44 Questions," and "A Newcomer Asks" are also available from AA.